HOMOCAUST

Exhausting the Burning Stick

VOLUME 1

Brian L. Jacobs

Dedicated

To my loving Husband, Thye Peng (Michael) Ngo for being a human of great inspirational action and pushing through all obstacles with his growth mindset;

Subsequently dedicated to all the other Queers, Dykes & Faggots out there, that absorb possibilities.

Homocaust:
Exausting the Burning Stick: Volume 1

In what I call a Rhizomatic Poetic, the unrooted pilgrim poet (and the reader as a sort of pilgrim writer through interpretation) rhetorically fills in elliptical meanings via envisaging metaphor, exploring diverse self-experiential contexts, imagining new universes in errantry, rupturing, mapping a-linearly, while proliferating without boundaries or centers in the margins of society without limits, rejecting principles of hegemonic, androcentric-arborescent roots, creating desire that is always in flux along new pathways of experimentation, manifesting into possibilities. This Rhizomatic Poetic inquiry explores diverse poetic acts based on a Pilgrimage I took walking for peace with Buddhist monks and other peaceniks halfway around the world from 1994 to 1995. I amplify, structure, and transform elements of my own experiences and "identity" into my poem, *Homocaust.* These original contributions are my poesies' discursive narratives mutating through exploring fractured memory, decolonizing the "self," Otherness, romanticization of the Other, and subsequently sometimes with elicit performances of queer identities overlapping Rhizomatic voices in errantry while discovering every possible elsewhere, while becoming my own liberating vehicle into fresh opportunities and possibilities. The arts, specifically poetics, may be the only medium to weave these complex tasks, making the Rhizomatic Poet the "true" auditor of our world.

Brian L. Jacobs

Acknowledgements

I extend my deepest gratitude to those who have journeyed alongside me, enriching this path with their unwavering support and encouragement. Andi Edson, my cherished companion and honorary "sister," provided the initial impetus for embarking on this endeavor. Without her steadfast belief in me, this journey would have remained but a distant dream. A serendipitous visit to my mother's abode, following adventures across the landscapes of Utah, ignited within me the resolve to return to poetic pursuits, an intricate tale too vast to fully recount here. My husband, Michael, who embarked on his own journey in Nursing, played an instrumental role in shaping my decision to rekindle my poetic pursuits. Amidst the tumultuous era ushered in by the onset of Covid-19 and Donald Trump, with time suddenly becoming a plentiful commodity, I found solace and purpose in the pursuit of knowledge. My heartfelt appreciation extends to my esteemed PhD supervisors, Dr. Alan Bilton, Dr. Alan Kellermann and Dr. Matt Hollrah, whose sage guidance and unwavering support served as beacons of light amidst the daunting expanse of this rhizomatic epic odyssey. In this intellectual peregrination, I have drawn sustenance from a myriad of visionary minds and creative luminaries. From the philosophical musings of Gilles Deleuze and Felix Guattari to the poetic brilliance of Audre Lorde and Edouard Glissant, each has left an indelible mark on my intellectual landscape. Special gratitude goes to Wanda, whose introduction to the works of Edouard Glissant sparked profound inspiration within me. The artistic tapestry woven by figures such as Reza Abdoh, Essex Hemphill and Marlon Riggs, alongside literary luminaries like Jack Kerouac, William S. Burroughs, and James Baldwin, has served as a wellspring of creative energy and intellectual stimulation. Their contributions have illuminated my academic journey, enriching it with depth and nuance. I am indebted to a pantheon of creative spirits, including Pedro Almodóvar, Keith Haring, and the trailblazing NEA Four (Tim Miller, Holly Hughes, John Fleck & Karen Finley), whose fearless expression has challenged societal norms and expanded the boundaries of artistic possibility. Their influence, alongside that of activists, musical and artistic maestros and others of influence like: Grace Jones, Boy George, Radiohead, PJ Harvey, Patricia Smith, Walt Whitman, The Beats, the Language poets, Lyn Hejinian, both the artist Nick Cave & the singer Nick Cave, Sam Rami, Jean Rhys, Erasure, House Music, The Smiths, Lee Edelman, John Waters, Lana Del Rey, Patti Smith, Michel Foucault, the American Visionary Arts Museum in Baltimore, Kurt Vonnegut, Sheila-Na-Gig Inc, ACT UP, Daniel Day Lewis, Zhang Huan, Arthur Danto, Derek Jarman , Kiki Smith, Marc Almond, Nina Hagen, This Mortal Coil, Bjork & The Sugarcubes, Divine, John Waters, Tracey Thorn,

Lady Gaga and Florence Welch. They resonate deeply within the fabric of my errant pursuits. I extend my heartfelt appreciation to a constellation of cherished friends whose unwavering support has been a source of immeasurable strength and inspiration. Geo, Rico, Liz, Anita, David, Ronan, Choong, Rochelle, Raju, Clara, Donna, Swani, Taci, Jojo, Gordon, Grace, Evan, Caitlin, Tierra, Eileen, Liana, Jay, Lisa, Cindy, Oktay, Chen, Ali, Jayme, Rubi, Jose, Nik, Zak, Christie, Alexander, Gene, Jeannie, Swani, alongside the LB Garlic Poets/Schoolmates and SABEH Crew; your presence has illuminated my path, enriching it with laughter, camaraderie, and boundless encouragement. To my beloved family, although not always perfect, whose unwavering love and support have opened doors to endless possibilities, I am eternally grateful for all that you have exposed me to in this insane life. And to the luminaries who have graced my life with their wisdom and kindness; Allen Ginsberg, Julie Patton, Anne Waldman, Kathryne McMahon, Clifton Snider, and Elyse Blankley. Your enduring presence continues to inspire and uplift me, infusing this journey with profound meaning and purpose.

Contents

Burnt Stick Pilgrim Itinerarium:
A Rhizomatic Prayer

Afoot and light-hearted I take to the open road -Walt Whitman

step into this body of peace

an isle of exile addicted to violence

un blessing me by the non gods in this cosmological bag

my poetic vertigo babel enroute to a new communal order of equals

unamalgamated contagions pilgrim'd in each pink step
an invitation to errant imprints

a privilege in anguish in an odor of vagabonds
where strangers congregate on shores of banishment

kept my charities of perversity vulnerable to my vestment

this Homocaust of mine *die endlosung der judanfrage homosexuell*

to chant imperviousness
amazes the ripening pods that hang afloat

carrying the seed spit considerable distances to my expulsion
on this paper tiger's moral geography

intersects in human and nonhuman ahimsas
on porous boundaries this terminus register of cantor articulation song

ruminates on a history of my persecution
for my poetics inadequate following atrocities

for how to go on living after Homocaust but in these writings
with steps towards clarity

queer clarity skipping rope with the reaper scribes poesy

these poetic screams transcend an extermination mass for the purpose of my healing

patch worked rhizomes meditating in phrontistery steps

schedules haphazard study in my torn jeans

sometimes these steps stumble diversely in unpredictable realms
question poetic L'Amours that task the savage ritual state

this narrative
not innocent

a guilty confederacy that should admit itself so
a prerequisite for denial

this hollowed temple body impious design
evinces nothing sacred or transcendental

base and plebeian leveling this rejected rectum of heroism
as I am an islet in Europe or maybe a cow

my body a non cell pilgrimaging souls fecundity
to my loving scars

flying peacocks with galloping antelope and drum charging oxen
lifting the throb at the avalanche pedestal

and in the shadow of the Beats
pilgrimaging into India's Samsaras

I can be
a cypress tree

if writers are whores I am a rhythmic complication
I am suburbia's Walt Whitman

a liquescent sift greased on counterfeit disposition
not missing the chance to listen to myself

for I am not a clock
but intricate hopscotch

even if this man sits at a blank page
it doesn't mean words suit this cosmogony

these trippings' steps
poems inhabited by spirits' ash heaps

colorful victims more present than the living word
against despondency offending libretto's authority

in need of talisman daring
captured by my own authority to relish in this errantry

witnesses are ugly whores I teach that dispute history
and go on about the inadequacies of this world

am I a citadel
liberated through the Baldwin house

those who do not know this peppermint set in platinum
must pray to death and beauty that glory and eternity can still toil the sow'r

the ulcers come aching
and obliterated amongst this sacred geography

this pilgrim
a consultation with dirt

hounded and neglected
in mutants of memory

as ash'd heretics are burned like stick fire on the faggot heaps
marking the unremarkable reified in my recenter

there is no self without this earth holding me down to do this work
I am an edit before death

burying my brethren burning tongue into blossom
I fall quiet

the drink of nightmares facing east west creating language illusions
as maps plowing divergent semantic turfs claiming the world I want to enter

a valediction to understanding soaks the creeping figs that resemble vaginas
or is it kidneys

the freeway has memory under poetry's frowns

so I walk unarmed pageants to mutate in a community minus strangers

a pilgrim called again to myself creating texture in my step compassions' scars
queering me dust

steps against uniformed killing industry
maps calling me to myself

fraught
the scarecrow immigrant whipped strawberry fields

planted near the orange groves of my suburban youth
and I step

Step I.

I never wanted a home nor a Lotus Sutra
I am not a lotus eater

I'm a rapture of rainbow assassins
formalisms' loss

I am a complex ask of fantast's accretion
floating in language soundfacts

Step II.

home is a place to hang history

a privilege created by language illusions

Step III.

I am a pilgrim palmate'd and spread
an intourist in the Derrida rings

where *Orpheus sings no more*
he writes

yes let's celebrate the contributions of brutal genocidal landgrabs
and chewing Earth's cartilage's poetic possessions of non myopic terrains

where adjectives are foreigners
and poetic biology hangs from the gallows of this writing table

rethinking the possible
concocting the protocols of clarity

who's wounded at which table I write
and where no dogma lives loudly

for this is not a complaint
it's a poem

Step IV. Possibility's Ode to Rhizomatic Pilgrims

wasteman hallow-land parataxis e tu
solipsism synecdoche metonymy green grass blue

the mango tree cannot bear lemons
god gunt coup

a doom loop of rivers flowing backwards
dongie dongie do

Step V.

I am a pilgrimaging Jacobipede
creating sacred space

I am not a hero
nor conquistador

just a fallacious queer map
a hero otherize'd budding errant exploits

Step VI.

dequeer me
unfaggot me

finish me off
the other ledger

Step VII.

I am not of heredity
I am called to errantry

I am not shaking things up from external pressures
not rising up from cavernous within

not fronting metamorphosis
not transmogrification

I am refusing your call
while not dreading the unknown

I am not turning away from errantry
there's no one mentor nor seasoned traveler

nor son heir
nor proficient sea to cross

no world's training
no equipment

no advice
nil's clutch within me

no cradle of valor and acumen
no crossing the threshold

no entering new regions
no conditions

no special world tests for all are special worlds with no catechism
no approach for it is all demand

and this ordeal
this pilgrim a collision confronting death

the end of your civilization

queer

Step VIII.

for it is at the womb where the rape started
at my birth the sacred geography defornicated

I am god's gunt
for I am a burnt stick pilgrim wounded at which table I write with dead Jews in the Danube

a witness
to the debris of mourning faggotry

deploying mirror bouquets exhausted eye bag witnesses
like replenished greedy testicles

Step IX.

embuggerance me and return me to dung
a battle ground of intestines exhausting this burning stick

a rainbow refugee of rainbow assassins

a fumigator

Step X.

the violence of Cypress California
suburban homespun degenerescence

Step XI.

an intourist flummoxed map to pilgrim'd language
Foucault's stubborn will to non knowledge is my Homocaust exhaustion

Holofernes vengeance
with Hejinian's *snakes and bees or wholly formed flowers*

grin hung around without the Foucault cat
and Rimbaud pees phantasmagorical

god is a cunt burnt stick pilgrim who's wounded at which table I write
ominously eclipsed in the thrush of my childhood

therefore
I step

Step XII.

into the pink triangle's math and color
naming it oxidized in the terror of my childhood faggotry

a strange pilgrim
a world wanderer looking for L'Amour

I am a faggot performer exhausting a burning stick
god's cunt gash reject in a Georges Bataille compost lazurustingly adrift in the Jain burial
sky

walking with peacocks' monkeys leaping gazelles
and Audre Lorde excrement's democracies

defining this wood stick
faggot incensed

Step XIII.

no hero recompense or possession
no danger of eluding the hero treasure

no road back
but rhizomatic

no home

no urgency

no resurrection
no purification

no resolve until dissolution
no elixir

no exegesis
no bearing

no power
no hero of land nor landscape in this performance faggotry

the sacrilege extending beyond boundaries of officially condoned beliefs and practice
no new empirical investigation queer

Step XIV.

walking creating sacred space
landscape's aura emanates fresh topographies

walkers encounter the landscape visually and materially engaged with it kinetically
sensually imaginative in this poetics

Step XV.

abandoned worldly conditions and the cosmos possessions forsaken in nation cities
temple bodies new identities superseding division imagining infinite volumes

no one can be content when the poetics refused you in the clamor
the right to obscurity opacity and noise

no immobiliti
no unity

no totality
queer

Step XVI.

can we raise a sun soaked yam
possibilities

Step XVII.

rhizomatic poetics is this Stradivarian note as queer as an exit from democracy
and like enmities blood voice de linking by crossing the brutality of borders militarized

a pilgrim borrows citizenship and forfeit's Pharmakon's occupation to chance
to exit the abyssal wall'd sleep of pain bodies

re symbol'd in castration
turning backs on the west

assignations of this queer burden
a mechanic communion

ebb dimensions agentas
in new sacrimentalize'd law

forced march in the hallucinatory dream of a community of strangers
a pilgrim

Step XVIII.

soilless vagabonds and delinquent tramps
ride

Step XIX.

a new divine
my divine's invocation code a subjectivity deceased

I am a foreclosed origin of non fellows
I am neutered exclusion

I am exiled sentences acclimatizing in regimes of heteronormativity
the enmity of nature

Step XX.

misprision me unnatural in inertia's secrecy
weave gambles and texture me the weave to entwine me no margins

Step XXI.

poetics necessity to mitigate suffering
for poetry is not innocent

it is guilty
a confederacy that should admit itself so

this poesy is nothing more than a reaction
a prerequisite for denial mitigating rhizomatically my suffering

Step XXII.

turbulent poetics' itinerarium a coexistence of multiple others
gold bar azeotropes' roaches in the mad state

refracted in a poetic sputum
hemorrhaging me and oystering me onto the open road

conquesting heredities' intolerant atrocities clotting thought that refuses my mot juste
unfurling shock into the marginal sassafras' den of this Lucretia

Step XXIII. Homocaust Pilgrimage Coda

heretic lesions landed on my ulcers as a uranists lagoon'd of my symbolic freight
fitting my sound suit

isolated and incensed in my poetic cum
an exhausted burnt stick I amen'ing

hanging from the baked oven gallows
of my errant poesy

Arborvitae:

Performance of The Burning of the Faggot Collectors; A Rhizomatic Renaissance

those luminous skulls among the rows of peas,
-and all the other phantasmagoria -Arthur Rimbaud

Open O' fierce flaming pit! Louis Zukofsky

Stick I.

Sati pyre phakelos yomiagne yells in all the light we cannot see
gather thee faggots and fly up wing'd achene's unsolfege'd fire bush exiled in stuprum's botany

at birth's dirge I face the faggots I gathered numb as angels' rejection
a blue print here for disintegrates

Allen Ginsberg up in flames
corpse me poetic dragged into Ronald Reagan death pits

where James Baldwin is Martin Luther Queen's comic eunuch
where Baldwin and Whitman marry testicles in hand

Stick II.

Varanasi vessels float the smoldering Ganga ghats metonymy with Audre Lorde up in flames
as primordial kindling under paradise's death box in my marriage bed

Stick III.

Stonewall burns Lex Scantinia fire
as tree omphalos vascularity is three worlds' amalgamation

androgyne wombed four hundred and thirty million years ago
during the Silurian period before vertebrates invaded with radiation adaptation

Devonian trees thirty meters high with woody stems
and no faggots to burn

Stick IV.

carboniferous spike moss
androcentric reproducing spore sperms

a mass extinction of me
where trees are colonize'd pilgrims

forests gymnosperms
naked seeded and arrested

where I am burned at the stake and the Haoma trees of dying gods knowledge eradicate inverts
with Walt Whitman up in flames

let the motherfucker burn Faustian
two hundred thousand ways to burn a fag

Stick V.

moses' bush daisies asters' sunflower lettuces
and skunkweed's eunuchs bear cone'd needle like evergreen

Stick VI.

the awl shaped thick fleshy stem
the broad deciduous fruit flowers

arborvitae's genesis
degenerated

adam adam eve eve
pink original sin

Stick VII.

small poles' posts lamb shepherd wing'd bottoms easily rubbed off
the scar's fruit winged seed in moist buds notch

tip silky axed woolly twigs of the heaven tree's sacred birds
appear'd branches to the coiled serpent

apple'd
and cored

Stick VIII.

white ash me in abandon my heavy wood grained plump blunt pointed
sati terminalizing the bud of drooping clusters ripe for serrations

pointed and notched
the sun of demonic Diti

Stick IX.

apex's toothed coarsely gnosis roots
sweet dew tree vanquishers witness Adonis' birth

quaking aspens burn soft weak

not durable incurved and fluttering in the lone leaves

Stick X.

fruit seed'd
prune'd liberation

Stick XI.

tufts of hair carried long distances by the wind creating a fabric on fag ash'd prairies
in ditches' remains mucilaginous chewed rope

bent but for floating sati ash of indistinguishable features
un opened parachute wounds

Stick XII.

American beech fagus grandifolia Ehrhart FAGUS placed here poetic
it has been left standing here a wasp nest as infects insect my injuries

62

Stick XIII.

gravelly petunia inconspicuous scrapings in my burnt elongated breathing
swimming fuel

faggot ash sati
floating the Ganga

Stick XIV.

erect verdures
fixed of other

Stick XV.

colonize disturbingly inferior interiors
aged dull and chalky white in my terminal rhetorics

Stick XVI.

The Susquehanna muddy winding current intolerantly spools resinous and impervious to water
burn'd a stout souvenir hunter's game

as our dear one James Baldwin is hunted and scorched
up in flames

Stick XVII.

die endlosung der Judanfrage homosexuell swamps sprout roten stumps
the ragged fringe fruiting performance

Mathew Shepard fence posts infected with canker disease
this quintessence of dust ripening his final solution

Stick XVIII.

black cherry in the murkiest opulent saturated bottomlands breathing pores
roughened upturned edges

68

gather ye faggots as ye may
ole fag ash a still a fly'n

Stick XIX..

the hydrocyanic acid bitter almond taste of rosaceae prunus dulcis plantae almondare ovate
winter buds

creating
is cyanide

Stick XX.

scarecrow Mathew Shepard's wild red cherry sati post
his sweet anus was divine

burned hallowed and abandoned on unStonewall'd lands
this Homocaust exhausting a burning stick

terminal and array'd peacock fence posts
slump'd scarecrow banquet for turkey vultures pickin'ing his ripe'd fruit

pickin'ing
his ripe'd fruit

Stick XXI.

lanceolate's flame
a pin cherry fire

midrib undersurfaces
a palpated single leaf

decidedly bitter in distinguished ember clusters
cultivated and abandoned on the hedgerow

a stranger
sprout'd resurrection wood

Stick XXII.

wilts tassel'd matted scarlet Hester Prynne

oblong'd veneer's graceful symmetry crown'd ornament atop the fire crowned faggots

Stick XXIII.

with lethal Dutch Elm Disease irresistant strains reign irregular
farrow blistering in fragrant oily resin borne rancid

as rosy hemlock pink
up in flames

Stick XXIV.

when the ripe disturbed fag fries prize'd in winter
goddess Harvey Milk up in flames

Stick XXV.

easily gnarled and craggy fleshes resinously coated and notched at the apex
a hickory taste and ash mouth filled heresy where borders become poofters

Stick XXVI.

pignut shagbark shallows the narrows and furrows detachedly
where Oswiecim ash pits bud

76

splintered rose like ascending stout flame'd limbs
where prosthetics' experiments are hobo Ronald Reagan pit fire fuel

Stick XXVII.

Dorothy's other Kansas
unshorn drag uprising

on the death of Dorothy's good good red slipper'd witch
Judy Garland dies June 22 1969

Stick XXVIII.

tamarack hackmatack fence posts
telegraph poles and railroad ties are lynchings' welcome

roughened wart like branches and fruit stalks
wind twists'up a black locust

Stick XXIX.

settlers' dooryard tree escaped dense thickets
the locust borers' warlock fags rendered worthless fuelwood

Stick XXX.

ripening pods hang sail
carry the spit seed considerable distances

my rectum a paper tiger of sweet honey locust
and Ganesha

a hardy and scattered traveler
a reader removed of obstacles

I am fagwood knotty kindler
a Jain sky burial vulture cloud in Gwalior

cum syrup of samaras' samsaras
striped thriving in the blazes subcanopy

with a dense understory the metanarrative distinguished
interlacingly spiraling as I choke on its islands of infestation

groomed for the gasses as ravines of disparities
my dense foliage unravels

Stick XXXI.

clefts between lobes shallow sharp
angled arcane clefts the brims of serrated sensibility

possibilities extinguished
a necromancer and occultist wing'd achene ripening in May or early June

as seeds diverge under the fire angels
and maenads with teeth in the Stonewall'd shade

deeply cut clefts
between coarse toothed lobes a ranker

crushed wing'd fruit
an *Angel in America* up in flames

Stick XXXII.

cross furrows rough ended in screams
people with AIDS up in flames

Stick XXXIII.

imprisoned buggered fartknocker
the end of democracy

whores' war warpaint
a syndrome Hester'd in scarlet oak

woolly meat immolation bereavement
a faggot up in flames at death's fragrant birth

Stick XXVIII.

cutting his tied body down with last rights from the fence post penitentiary
shadbush serviceberry ascending the rivers and crossing the Rubicon

84

baptized in the River Jordan on doses of Sadhu hash cakes
while bathing with cows in the Ganga sourwood

faggots burn poetic
on papyrus

Stick XXXIX.

lignum vitae's incensed the ten percent
millions ablaze

Stick XL.

blueprint for burning fags
use hardwood slow growing deciduous trees

trees with loose leaves
logs of greater density and heavier project more heat output

hacked wood logs schemes with moisture content of less than twenty percent
clack them together loudly rather than a dull thud is ideal

wood seasoned outdoors between eighteen to twenty four months
best for a good fag burn

the harder the wood the longer the seasoning
hallowed stacked off ground with plenty of space between allow air movement

with no rain and no snow for seasoned wood gives you fifty percent more heat
to put out output makes it very worthwhile

as they denaturalize emancipately exclusionary
a moisture meter highly recommended a small tempered investment

hard wood ash birch beech oak and elm
for best results flaming the queens

avoid burning woods with a high resin
heavier wood the deader the fags

apple wood burns slowly and steadily
with reasonable heat a lovely smell

however it produces a disappointing flame
not pink in Eve's provision a commodity

with Ash Dieback disease having a devastating impact on ash trees
torch your faggots disease free

make sure your wood is not legally restricted like Clause 28
ash log firewood may only be moved off these infected sites with Forestry Commission authority

get a faggot permit
with a pleasing pink perfumed smell

cedar produces a well burning log
long lasting heat

lovely slow burning cherry wood
producing a good heat output as well as a lovely smell great at Christmas faggot crucifixions

eucalyptus has obviously pleasant aromatic smells
and burns reasonably well with Larry Kramer up in flames

laburnum poisonous nasty sulfurous yellow sap oozes inordinate amounts of foul smelling
smoke makes good kindling especially in high heels

Greg Louganis too wet to burn
producing sparks and pink smoke

yew slow burns with tremendous heat
but soot and creosote so cowl the faggots before incinerating

blackening lackluster with dull dirty firebricks of Fire Island Shangela
acquired immunodeficiency syndrome

arborvitae's patient zero
a Ronald Reagan's bonfire

Stick XLI.

Wittgenstein's fire separating us from other animals
Ludwig Wittgenstein up in Flames

smother a fire with a blanket or sand
Ioves lightning strikes Zeus

charcoal a fag as partially combusted material
it's a Stonewall riot!

copious faggots gasses grasses and grasslands
as savannas fire stick farm to scrub this faggoty forest rhizomatic

exterminations' charred final solutions
ambushed opportunistic light

insect us away in ancient hearths
faggots roasting like meat

Stick XLII.

time for Rhizomatic Poetics
flints' tool kits for heretics

Stick XLIII.

wildfire
galactic faggot narratives

Stick XLIV.

witches and burned faggots oil dipped afire
in the faggot light of the burning pyre with *the love that dare not speak its name* up in flames

91

inquisition witches cooked at the purse and aniconic faggot aflame'd on the Siddhartha wheel
with lamentations sprinkled pepper tree in gold and saffron robes

Stick XLV.

fan the flames after sun bake and shake bake in ball of fire out of the frying pan into the fire blaze a trail blow smoke up your ass body heat bra burner brand new fire place fire side chat in heat in the heat of battle wavy lines rays in the line of fire

burn after reading burn a hole in your pocket burn in hell burn rubber grate looting

burn the midnight oil burn up the track burn your bridges burn the candle at both ends

burn yourself out burning desire Chinese fire drill crash and burn fire and rain

burning issue burst into flames c'mon baby light my fire catch fire smoke screen carry a torch for dead heat hearthstone fire sale consuming burnt to a cinder

don't burn your bridges behind you draw someone's fire burned at the stake burning down the house energy to burn Fahrenheit 451 feel the burn fiddling while Rome burns fight fire with fire double double toil and trouble fire burn and cauldron bubble

fire down below fire engine red gas lighted get on like a house on fire burning in me

fire in the hole liar liar pants on fire fire away great balls of fire fire sale

friendly fire sweat lodge mustard seed hearth redemption fire the imagination glow little inch worm glow go out in a blaze of glory agni verdic fire god fire in your belly fire storm go through fire go up in flames go up in smoke glow with health throw fuel on fire have many irons in the fire heat up heat wave lady of fire heap coals of fire first hire and last fired hold a torch torch song trilogy holy smoke ride the solar lamb I love the smell of napalm in the morning if you can't stand the heat get out of the fire keep the home fires burning kindling fire and brimstone it burns me up brush fire light a fire under him like a moth to a flame I got a burning desire for you baby fire back money to burn my ears were burning on the back burner on the front burner open fire packing heat torch bearing alchemic baptism by fire barn burner pat a cake pat a cake baker's man bake me a cake as fast as you can flash burn gun fire piss like a fire engine play with fire in the heat of the moment put that in your pipe and smoke it ring of fire second degree burns set the world on fire slash and burn slow burn smoke around the campfire smoke like a chimney smoke out someone ears are burning swallow your own smoke the nth degree there's no smoke without fire third degree wheel's on fire throw another log on the fire too many irons in the fire turn up the heat under fire where there's smoke there's fire where's the fire white heat stabilizer the heat is on purity lion's mane set your hair on fire s'mores light bulb lightening menorah Hanukkah lights baked Alaska creme brulee say their names fire starter gas chamber oven geo thermal energy geysers solar

hot take hot pocket hot topic burn the dj smoke and mirrors restore primordial

the roof the roof the roof is on fire we don't need no water let the motherfucker burn

burn mother fucker burn hot stuff hell Westboro Baptist Church red hots flume

spicy hot fire storm fire starter your mother sucks cocks in hell disco inferno Dante's Inferno Paris is burning mirage heat rises demonic devouring flames

volcanic sunrise sunset burn in hell cat on hot tin roof hot chocolate blaze of glory

fired up ready to go sunburn mouth on fire grilled cheese throw them on the fire

summer heat shrimp on the barbie brined churrasco burning up for your love

cuz I'm on fire heartburn unforgettable fire hot as hades river Styx smoke pipe

ring around rosey the gagging ashes goblet of fire courage under fire camp fire

backdraft ablaze fire house fire station into the fire chariots of fire tetrahedron fire ant red hot chili peppers fire comet leave the light on apocalypse fiery

candle in the window bang bang fire fire fighter fire brigade corona fury

fire extinguisher fire alarm fire fight fire exit flame thrower dance around the fire grease fire fire torch dancers playing with fire blood shot red eyes down in flames

hairdresser on fire house fire don't touch the stove fire walk with me fire roasted crack pipe chimney candle in the wind screaming fire in a crowded theater

Stick XLVI.

fire island up in flames
patient zero up in flames

in the power of the sun's impregnation destruct
and the kali yuga luminary fire tongue wags

Stick XLVII.

ambulatory this frosty sunup stump in the wet grassland
pleasure laments with two bearded kisses

before the morning faggot collection he is tethered and followed
to amass the twiggiest drizzliest rhizomatic twigs

I am dragged with him in requiem to the marshaled bulk of faggots tied with contempt
clothed in abhorrence Ronald Reagan

they light the match with jeers
the toes smell first before the bearded kisses

as the dermis evaporates amongst the holler in this emerald faggot timbered arena ash
blooms trying to bloom in un bloom'd burnt blackened pastures' arborescence

Stick XLVIII.

I must leave you now
the smell of permanence

95

the smell smell of rose water
they will chant you a smell of crushed grapes

the smell of dried lime
you have boxed your talents L'Amour

you smell of patchouli soap
our smell is a bouquet of mirrors

you will call me by your name
I will smell you to my grave

in that marriage bed
gardenia lavender wisteria

Stick XLIX.

fagat fagete, fagett fakettes fakettis faget faggett faggott ffagott fagot faggit faggat fagget fagott faggot facket facket fagget faggett fakket vaggot faggit fagela fagattis faggat, fagget faggottis fagotes fagatus fagettus fagottus fagotus fagotto fangotto

fag

Stick L.

for your scorch bundle the sticks
sati the bugger'r

Stick LI.

as double negation around mold's orbit during the fall into twoness as state unsanctioned sodomy
performing it Homocaust

Stick LII.

The knight von Hohenburg and his squire pyre
Pompeii'd volcanic stone direction cement cock brothel'd in funerary urns

cremations induced exchanges
diagenesis turning to ash

suffocate restricted oxygen in the septic sky
tissues contract in curled pugilistic poses calcined reduced porosity

increased crystallinity
calcined Jodie Foster up in flames

Stick LIII.

Rome's Lex Scantinia inforced stuprum condemned
court ordered castrated and burned between the thighs

a renaissance bardassoes boys
pink'd pogroms a blood wedding

latched at their beingness
the fruits due ripening

thunder shakes
the un aegis' jail

innumerable spaces
Chechnya blazes

USA USA
USA!

Stick LIV.

how inadequate poetry is to this rhizomatic task
me up in flames

Stick LV.

Pulse Orlando Nightclub up in flames
Presidents of the United States of America faggot regimes

act up fight AIDS
this queer nation up in flames

Stick LVI.

Vimal means clean in Hindi
locked me in a room

the women sleep downstairs and shit with the pigs
a coercive polemic cataclysm

him entering my rectum
war painted melancholia against my butt cheeks

I bathe in plastic rickshaw wash buckets
this is how I get clean

rectum up in flames
his name was Vimal

Stick LVII.

Haze'd limp wrists direct them to burn burn burn the witch
gay panic edict don't drop the soap

in your Twinkie defense
Milk

a fag's place hangs under the boot
Nietzschean affirmation as a farewell to understanding

you must soak the vine that is slithering in Eve's Eden
Oscar Wilde up in flames

bruised pink and lavender under the death bureaus
with people of Lot becoming sexed *Yehareg ve'al ya'avor*

die rather than transgress
hazing candles manhood this grammar that structures me

a burnt tree seeded fruit rhizomatic sodomite
this unfit scapegoat does not fit the androcentric matrix in my unmasked Joan of Arc

the end of democracy
the private space of your rectum

police arrive at the Stonewall Inn 1969
erotic fates

Leonardo Da Vinci
up in flames

Stick LVIII.

I am a Third Reich outlaw
don't ask don't tell

I am written in Paragraph 175
a moral crusaders cabaret bent gassed and interned

a rainbow minority report
Kristallnacht

arrests deemed tinder before the masses
I am 3A artificial male sex hormone implanted

lobotomized
drowning in immolation piss regimes

Stick LIX.

evergreen re education program
electro shocks the fictive everpink

churches the holly phallus
out of you

Stick LX.

clinging to one other
today's Pulse's parody

our modernity's trees
Reza Abdoh up in flames

Stick LVII.

gather the cylindrical bundle of twigs to ignite
let the motherfuckers burn

Harry Hay Greg Araki Shangela Alexander the Great Marsha P. Johnson Hatshepsut Cherrie Moraga Gene Genet Paula Gunn Allen K.D. Lang Anohni Nathan Lane Bruce LaBruce Our Lady J David LaChapelle Edward Albee Guayin Rimbaud Paul Verlaine Eureka O'Hara Gianni Visace Perfumed Genius Leonardo da Vinci Jane Lynch Mj Rodriguez Indya Moore B.D. Wong Pedro Zamora Angelica Ross Dan Choi Countee Cullen Larry Kramer Jane Wagner Alexander Wang George Michael Lorraine Hansberry Isaac Mizrahi Neil Tennant Tennessee Williams Montgomery Clift Nahkane Alice Walker Walt Whitman A foot and light hearted I take to the open road Rudolf Nureyev Gore Vidal Cynthia Nixon Sandra Bernhardt Matt Lucas Rupaul Jim Nabors John Cameron Mitchell Mika Vergil Jane Velez Mitchell Rosie O'Donnell Langston Hughes Vaslav Nijinski Ryan Murphy Harvey Firestein Mary Oliver Eve Sedgwick Kelly McGillis Alan Turing Jean Marais Niecy Nash Luis Alfaro Freddie Mercury James Baldwin Armistead Maupin Derek Jacobi Wilford Owen Eileen Myles Tab Hunter Neal Cassady Linda Hunt Terrance McNally Kristy McNichol Alexander McQueen Tiger king Janelle Monae Johnny Mathis Audre Lorde Robert Mapplethorpe Klaus Nomi Boy George Ian McKellen Kate McKinnon W. Somerset Maugham Janis Joplin Moms Mabley Rachel Maddow Clive Barker Fred Schneider Thomas Mann Kate Pierson Dan Levy Greg Louganis Michelangelo Billie Jean King Isaac Julien June Jordon Marlon Riggs Adam Lambert Reza Abdoh Little Richard Barbara Gittings Frank Ocean Esssex Hemphil Judy Baca Francis Bacon Clay Aiken Tim Miller Martina Navratilova Liberace Sally Ride Pete Buttigieg Keith Haring Quintin Crisp Jonsi John Waters Judy Grahn Marga Gomez Kate Clinton Lipsynca Harvey Milk Orlando Cruz Gloria Anzaldua Jackie Goldberg Judy Gold Stephen Fry E.M. Forester Rob Halford Tim Gunn Rupert Everett Ani DiFranco Stephanie Miller Andrea Dworkin Lee Edelman Joe Orton John Addington Symonds (my great grandfather's name John Symonds) Tom Ford Andy Bell Ronan Farrow Elton John Michel Foucault Delta Lambda Phi Judith Butler David Hockney Tammy Baldwin Dior Chirs Colfer Lea DeLaria John Cage Divine Victor Garber Melissa Etheridge Truman Capote Jean Cocteau Robin Roberts Chaze Bono Rock Hudson Beth Ditto Guiltier Richard Chamberlain Sia Adrienne Rich Lil Nas X B. Ruby Rich Don Lemon Graham Norton Wilson Cruz Vito Russo Saphire Ellen DeGeneres Freddie Mercury Anderson Cooper Dustin Lance Black Wanda Sykes Andy

Warhol Lou Reed Stephan Sondheim Lord Byron John Fleck Robert Rauschenberg Sarah Paulson Annie Sprinkle Socrates Alice B. Toklas Neil Patrick Harris Kenzo Dan Savage Kristen Stewart Lily and Lana Wachowski Wallace Stevens Darren Star Cecil Taylor Mathew Shepard Tchaikovsky Lily Tomlin Peaches Neruda Leonard Bernstein Abraham Lincoln Liz Smith Sylvester Barney Frank Gertrude Stein David Hyde Pierce Susie Bright Kaitlin Jenner Bayard Rustin Marquis De Sade Jimmy Sommerville Miss Coco Peru Anthony Perkins Lorca Sam Smith Ludwig Wittgenstein Pee Wee Herman Mary Daly Raven Symone Ma Rainey Derek Jarmen Pedro Almodovar Nate Silver Gus Van Sant Billy Porter Oscar Wilde Pete Burns Morrissey Plato Zachary Quinto Marc Almond Marcel Proust Ellen Page Jim Parsons Linda Perry Steve Kornacki Randy Rainbow Kathy Acker Allen Ginsberg Jodie Foster Cole Porter Bob the Drag Queen

Stick LVIII.

exhausting a burning stick in recanted heresy mark of shame
fry a faggot a bundle of reeds

metallurgy's thin strip peel wrapped in caul fat filth
uselessness slatternly bent

mischievous child polluted vagaries
burning perverted libertine violators re membered and assembled pink

libidinal drives suppress genital neurosis as ononisms' penetration welding
echolalias transcendent personhood disavowed glossolalias' metanarrative disambiguation

Michelangelo's Sistine Chapel
up in flames

ascension above the pyre
annexation in the colonial widow clouds of fag dust

the poetic yomiagne's fire yells
yoni yoni linga linga

Sticks LIX.

poesis
I that name arborvitae

LX. Rhizomatic Faggots: Exhausting a Burnt Stick

as the sun sets burn schemes of topographical revulsion
I become illicitly unloved in the soupy field's termagant moist mud

an ankle deep harpy
viscus sun browned

medieval and fetid pestilential baroque on the mound ropes' doomed targe
in the loathsome brackish stagnant sodden sod

knee deep as all-pervading ominous beasts
demand death in the hard baked arborescent muck

with pythoness hordes thaumaturge's finale
my magnum opus

reason abandon of the gallows herd and somber enchantment's hex
necromancer in these killing fields plant the seed and harvest your own wood

the faggot gatherers
cut with ax

felling deliming crosscut debarked logs chip away and saw gather fag poles for Mathew
sawn
throw prose into the fire

clear cut and transport the fags and harvest the chipper wood pulp
to burn the faggot

our audience
are auditors of queer identity

*Jesse Helms Ronald Reagan Popes Michele Bachman Putin Pat Robertson Donald J Trump
Police Robert Mugabe Westboro Baptist Church Dan White and his damn Twinkie John
Briggs (fuck this guy seriously) Sean Hannity Tammy Faye Phyllis Schlafly Parents The John
Birch Society Exodus International 700 Club Marcus Bachmann Anita Bryant Boy Scouts of
America Antonin Scalia Lyndon LaRouche Bob Jones Michael Savage Ron DeSantis Jerry*

performance faggotry up in flames
this poem up in flames

poetics up in flames
Brian Lynn Jacobs up in flames

Coda (Afterburn): Arbormortum

burned human remains
my muscles' tissues

skin blood arteries veins blood clots
blocking blood flow as veins melt destroying my circulatory system

the inner organs destroyed and die from smoke and heat inside and out of my corpse
flares down my airway postmortem fracturing

fragmentation's fire lips
lacuna burnt remains perimortem trauma totally destroy the body

victim identification through facial features
fingerprints dentistry Brian Lynn Jacobs

fatal fire scene recovery
analysis of body and burned skeletal elements

combust after placing the burning tire around the neck with fuel
and light it on fire head in flames necklacing faggots

rubber tire filled with petrol over chest and arms with a match spark charred
graphesis deployed gradual oxidation and exposure to the decay of hoary trees

modification of external skin
blisteringsplittingdisassociationflexureretraction

Minimataesque
Hiroshima

detachment of crucified hands
and distal radius and ulna exposed with feet detached

differentiated warpage as the detached bad faith other
James Baldwin is the fire god brahman and bodhisattva

a window appeared in the thorax detached
androgyne adrenaline's santorum

this body vessels emptied agent
gaze gasoline'd accelerant in the extremities

oh L'Amour
l'More

life threatening rainbow amputations
firstsecondthirdfourthfifthsixthdegreeand

faggots explosive inflammatory response
AIDS a gay cancer

destroy the problem contain the damage
clean up the mess Icarus hubris

weaken the immune system for the body is less able
to fight off threats of Reagan Salem's sepsis

gather the faggots to make much of time
gather ye faggots while ye may

old rainbow is still a flying
this same faggot that smiles today

tomorrow will be dying
Cherrie Moraga up in flames

arborvitaecaust crucible's
plague nation

Bridget Bishop June 10, 1692
Rebecca Nurse July 19, 1692

Sarah Good July 19, 1692
Elizabeth Howe July 19, 1692

Susannah Martin July 19, 1692
Sarah Wildes July 19, 1692

George Burroughs August 19, 1692
George Jacobs Sr. August 19, 1692

Martha Carrier August 19, 1692
John Proctor August 19, 1692

John Willard August 19, 1692
Martha Corey wife of Giles Corey

Mary Eastey September 22, 1692
Mary Parker September 22, 1692

Alice Parker September 22, 1692
Ann Pudeator September 22, 1692

Wilmot Redd September 22, 1692
Margaret Scott September 22, 1692

Samuel Wardwell Sr. September 22, 1692
Giles Corey September 19, 1692

erasure oh l'amour
mon amour

what's a boy in love
supposed to do?

L'More's phobic regime
Open O' fierce flaming pit!

Oh L'Amour: My Bruise'd Juvenile Tormentor

**L'More: Tormentor Archetype*

...each and every identity is extended through a relationship with the Other -Edouard
Glissant

*If I didn't define myself for myself, I would be crunched into other people's fantasies for me
and eaten alive.*-Audre Lorde

...metaphor measures distance as surely as identification -Lee Edelman

I tell you I have created this thing out of the squashed cabbage leaves- George Bernard
Shaw

*You're a lover. Borrow Cupid's wings and use them to soar higher than the average man. I
am too sore enpiercèd with his shaft To soar with his light feathers, and so bound, I cannot
bound a pitch above dull woe. Under love's heavy burden do I sink.*
-William Shakespeare's Romeo and Juliet

I. Punch

My name inhaled marked for extinction
from L'More my own personal dictator

so I walk pilgrimaged with phantasm's appetite of memory as an act of endurance
and who's mights aphorism's anonymities are distrusted by the unfathomable queer creation

in me not a pastime
nor a spectacle of sentiments nor aesthetic objects

but words impart habit to a realization that could certainly not be afflicted
by permanent desuetude

II. Hit

I am a ruffian afar and canonized at this paper
one who has subjugated the organism of alliteration

a Whitman lobotomist L'More
untangled resolute insignia

an enigma's prodigious summation of damnation's sinful castigation
love's chrystalization in poesy's rhizomatic vomit

an enticement of objectification excrement for the machinist's advantage
in L'More's methodical sutured un poem'd dermis incomes me

a mislaid map on poetics' path
and despite his velocity this contrivance is not chemistry nor splicing nor assemblages'

indeterminacy of adages' noumenon
for sutures be damn'd damned

L'More
you are my bruised innermost juvenile tormentor

III. Blow

we are both other L'More as amalgamation's vehement impurity
your rectum finger fucked hole ends democracy

as poetics' exorbitant order
restrained designs that do not endure traditions and abandon our celibacies

de assembling these facts and asserting hollows that supplant their composition
for ingenuity is infinitely free from all genuineness

IV. Shot

L'More used to fuck girls with Ziplock bags
L'more wanted me to un appear as I am cognition contagion

for L'more to reconstitute the organic pointillistic normative of collective anxieties
the slovenliness and barbarism in sheltering his anal pleasure

V. Jab

L'More we are friction's fictions between condescending languages
and our bond is domination

my performances are impoverishments
and I am annihilated sufferings of your learnt expressionary nonsense

a struggle eternally in my identity
in our chemicalled windbag'd otherness

we are both Jekyll Hyde confined L'More
empty to the transparent world you are used to running

L'More's holy universal opaque existence
where we all agree to endure

with and amid the other with no fusion
un capable of transcending alienation

L'More's terror and degenerative torment
of my famines' internments of abandonment and sequestration

and L'More's supercilious dominances of status quo's blind numb maintenance
in his rectal padlocked ideologies

L'More's poetic illiteracy
absent of splendor springs instability and de poesy'd

the more L'More regiments into stupor's office the more arousal of
consciousness'waywardness this rhizomatic pilgrim

L'More's anus of turbulent refusal
L'More's manufactured mythos of consent

adorns my alienation
queer

no nocturnal conflagration
a deteriorating negation of poetics' dearth for I'm in your shadow of being L'More

L'More's myopic pandemonium avaricious control
L'More's refutation contraption of vulgar proxies' clamor

what L'More doesn't know about his anus
is that knowledge is boundless

L'More's struggle against reductive thought disindividuates me
positivist's reduction in L'More's nationhood

wrapped up in his rectal pleasure quaking homophobic consequences
L'More's hierarchical exclusion transplanted terror anxiety upon me

a Faustian contract of heterosexual subordination of the other
exclusive negative and exclusionary

a taught preemptive and violent circumscription
both others not outside the language that structured me

we are para critique critiques side by side as false axioms should be of rhizomatic flow
not rooted and rejuvenating new resolutions

to a new map of rhizomatic dimensions and directions with a reaction to rationalism
freed from linear thinking

his text other me in my liberation
L'More my auditor of queer identity

VI. Knock

the poetic desired truth and the land that always seemed removed
from underneath my suburban feet is a blue print for degenerates
125

Shakespeare' hell is empty
and the devils are here in this 1984's *1984*

there is no self but art

without thinking about thinking without the earth holding me down boring desire out of me

I follow the path and don't talk to Hejinian wolves
L'More *I'll through celery* to your grave

VII. Slug

when optimism and memoire rhyme
birth's PTSD closets mutes my marginal actuality

and my cramped repudiation of convention in corporeal immoderations
placate subjugations' agent to assemble in poetics' emancipational might in the heaves of chaos

VIII. Smack

subtraction is key
L'More

the salt no sea
the other without other

changed by others' changes
the other adorned in motion's wretchedness and suspension with predetermined thoughts

disposedly transmuted into a mad state of inherited sterile infirmities of dependence of thought
without coaxing me public

without mutating me
inside the private gaze of your rectum register my terminus of your pleasure

IX. Belt

L'More exchanges in a violent partnership of filial legitimate hidden conquests
through his intolerances eliciting reciprocated embargoed rhizome humdrum descension

as my alienation L'More unmechanizes my world
and creates it un poetic arborescence

I swim amongst the evil genies
delinked in society's enmity gaze of democracy's egress

X. Bash

dis'ubuntu unwrapped in L'More
yet his only aim is my vanishing

my ruin
my occupation

my extraction
my perdition

my namelessness
my institutionalization

my extermination our division's exiting indifferences
my pain body circulating castration's orbit

this violent queer burden exposed
obstructing my desire to love L'More

while weakening faculties are ethical agents in Stockholm syndromes
divested possibilities

and bereft annals with poetic vivacity revivalism
L'More's squalid subordinate Eden

constricting my serpent in the colonized world
a technocrat demobilizing a regulatory agent

in L'More's constricted kingdom of departure proliferating discontent
for his hole's rapture be positioned drudgery onto other

pleasure's extraction removed like a pogrom'd pilgrim
a stranger

an alien

queer this pilgrim strange

destined for mutations' occupation and pillage

reified as humanity aimlessly wanders

L'More's liquescent shadow repeoples as subjectivity's foreclosed executioner

devouring and dissimulating the violent monopoly of internalization and bad faith constraints

self-preserving appeasements in this faggot performance spank as a burnt stick pilgrim's

filigree snail line sidewalks a black cat glow and disappears in hates diaspora

L'More's violent potency rituals' violently supplanted regulating comportment body

closes the door to release excrement

fearing the public rectal liberating expulsion

he so represses in his tyrannical monarchical gaze of me

XI. Slap

L'More self disciplining for the other may witness his rectal pleasure
and he joins the league of non fellows to burn the queer

Viva L'Rectum!
Viva L'Nation!

Those without part have no rights
and join the community of pilgrims' departures

XII. Pelt

When shitting L'More stops at the threshold of the othersphere
his excreting privateness publicly executes abject degradation pacifying mores

L'More's peace inflicts violent atrocities to establish strongholds of fear
not to comprehend his private pleasurable excrement release

I have something L'More does not
anal pleasure

so thwarting inception thus violently extorting cruel violence on others
L'More's systemic brutality and torture

burn the faggots at the stake
L'More's lack of anal pleasure corrupts his freedom body

thus imposing stringent norms of repressed intimacy for himself
to guarantee his utopian supremacy and provocation of repressed mobilization

affirming his class of sovereignty over faggots
maintaining principled preeminence

by destroying anal pleasure and sequestering compromising entanglements
of sphincter jouissance

XIII. Pummel

internal amalgamation's decrees of exclusion served neutered and exiled conquests
constitutes genocidal annihilation

L'More's manifested regime traipsing against the enemy of his destined nature
and his state duty to wage war on me

rectal white flags constrain his shit and his extermination elimination thrill
placing other outside of law

occupying my public rectal pleasure
refuting and obliterating all traces of his anal inclinations

originating in un law's uses of language
to oppress others alternative histories of humanity's transformed conception

unearthing the dissimilar
and less than mine never embracing the unaccepted pleasures of ramming cock

in your ass L'More
in mine

as a manifesto for imagination's fugitive unconscious memories
breathe poetic in your deprivation of vulgar pleasure's leaden repressed ignorance

knowing yourself as a segment
in the hollers of the unruly horde

XIV. Prod

I cry out for poesy's hedonism held together by opposites
to publicly discover himself without the antagonism on the other

open up the stall door L'More
the discovery for your essentialist problems

other me and make it impossible to find legitimacies in my performance
stop negating anal pleasure L'More

rocket Sylvester at your Studio 54 agent
un conquistador those who bear injustices at community's consent

and exile the voyage out of this anal enclosure
where territorial intolerances stop and distrust the fathomless world poetic

led nowhere in this cosmological rhizome
and *to thine own self be* faggot

inhale your injustice L'More of others' indiscernibles
and renounce certainty of a universal model for you rightfully can't escape your lack of control

XV. Dig

L'More you are explorer discovering queer knowing
the other is within us as the silence of the world in turn makes us deaf

with the aim of providing legitimacy to the attempt at domination
where L'More's empire is the shock of elsewhere

a renunciation of the earth and nature
and never become fixed in an already evident infinite possible elsewhere

XVI. Bop

In front of L'More's pure arrogant rigidity I squat in my faggot tag circle
drawn around this narrator crossing borders' rings

to clip the insinuations in genuine truancy
becoming redundant limpidity fixated on veiling your rectal pleasures

with tenant and pilgrim living the same exile
our circuits part naive of our disavowal not ruled by history

unaware of us as we
L'More diminishing this other to the pellucidities

quantified by one's performance
as I shit pleasurably

XVII. Knock

oh assimilated other
my annihilation generalized

we are same
yet other

crucified communal consent of legitimacies quest of the outright elimination of other
and excrement with elimination of sacred

anal pleasure as territorial conquest
believe L'More that you are knowledge's master but we are not one in the same perversion

within your dreaded dominate powers legitimacy blooms secretly planted in camouflage's pot
in unforeseeable viciousness' delusional insufferable exchange

of this apartheid for survival without neglected indulgences detour his digressions
for in the other's gaze we are destined inextricable knots delighting in our helixes

goaded annulled
decaying me fallen into immovable functions of rectal décor pleasures'

melancholy transmuting progression
while dehumanizing my voice not shaken but spoken

XVIII. Clip

structural weakness befalls L'More's potency penetrating anal secrecies
fucking with natural order

obstructing his orbits un natural
vailed in a thousand costumes

subversive anal undigestible exegete
grabbing and choking me other

XIX. Box

my blood book covered and opened
raking the leaves inside this house

repeat repeat repeat
non stop squirting American apple pie out my ass

while squated over the American flag singing out of tune Nancy Reagan
just say yes yes yes L'More

XX. Strike

L'More
my home is a jail body

L'More for out of my sight you live in this house
carrying the ruined city seed spit under my skin yet not careful with my burden

mark it L'More
place it in the land of exile'd strangers

in our own bodies
halloo'd in the chasms reverberating of other

betraying
queerness

rules of our inextricable in the othered toxic paradise as dominations assertivenesses
and falsities as provider as protector and controller

privileges in enshrined authority
L'More

more than faggot
publicly un queer

XXI. Knockout

L'More's mystic hole
sceptered copulatory gland

his boy pussy
a rep for the law in its state of poverty of pleasure

L'More fails to seize on his hole's creativity and poesy
an inmate in his own house

father's blood an heir to his authority
anatomized in his aesthetic pleasure gaze by looking at castrated fear of not having

and the pleasure derived of a respectable excretion
reflected in the rectal desideratum mirror

phantasmagorical queer un signifies your manhood L'More
your cum bullet in my mouth your castrations' mastery

I am isolated in poetics'cum of ceaseless differentiation
cursed and defeated

demolished my performance of steel clad identities
as James Baldwin shades occlude L'More's fetishization of phallus

and his anal protection spies surveillance in his paranoia
faggots here be dragons til' the end of earth

turn to fucking faggots L'More
for you are my muse and voice here in this rhizomatic poetic

protector of your anus and democracy's Jesus
loosening sphincter control

a Homocaust's hermaphrodism of the soul for L'More we are both human boys
in the natural order of disorder's trauma

pilgrimaging
in wander

XXII. Lollop

L'More master my other abrasions malady
rewarded perpetual spirals of power and pleasure with supremacy

moore'd to uncover anal pleasure
and this peculiar pervert mirrors your castration bruised pink lavender

a single drop of Achilles weak heal is compassion
Narcissus others himself gazing at his own reflection

lipsticked at the suicide kiss
Chrysippus' tutor Laius' rape

and Hermes' crocus flower at Pan's erect cock and oversized scrotum
Dionysus' intersexed

Heracles cauterized Hydra heads tear Orpheus apart maenads
Bacchic orgy Hermaphroditus' Amazonian clits and taints

and Teiresias' ballroom poses
Athena Myrmex's love plowed into ant

Aphrodite's Sappho and Eros plebicolist wing'd erotes
the regard of L'More's Iris sphincter

Iphis heterosexual death's farewell to understanding and L'More's phallophobia
my aversion to masculinity

L'More's Homocaustial fear
in the gut atoms' intestine inverted gunt

XXIII. Buffet

Patti Smith *The boy looked at Johnny, Johnny wanted to run,*
But the movie kept moving as planned

The boy took Johnny, he pushed him against the locker,
He drove it in, he drove it home, he drove it deep in Johnny

The boy disappeared, Johnny fell on his knees,
Started crashing his head against the locker,

Started crashing his head against the locker,
Started laughing hysterically

When suddenly Johnny gets the feeling he's being surrounded by
Horses, horses, horses, horses

Coming in in all directions
White shining, silver studs with their nose in flames,

He saw horses, horses, horses, horses,
horses, horses, horses, horses.

I am a living crime scene and a living hate crime
A small town boy

I place my rhythm tongue in L'More's sphincter
L'More wriggles and screams *horses horses horses horses horses horses*

dequeering in his dominance but I eat wing'd serpent fruit as fire screams in his pleasure
and I screech *horses horses horses horses horses horses*

as he punches me and threats a virus fucker training my transtemporal memory's performance
with neigh utterances resting pleasurably on my psychological furniture

XXIV. Cuff

L'More's cock
mot juste

L'More
bury me a pink grave

bury me in a river of Sylvester for my cells are paper poets
useless in the city state

L'informatique lightening
erected on the margins of contamination

with odorous vagrants and poetic skeletons
fashioned design in my performance faggotry

with L'More falling into twoness
and his repudiation of anal love masks his denials twice loss

denying opaquely
wanting comprehension

and never existing different
while threatening to become exile's punishments

XXV. Uppercut

other exiled
I forbidding foreboding's possibility of love
146

capitalized absence in my un male performance
L'More sex assigns me of what I have never been all along

the moment of construction in my public pleasure hole
mise en scene qualifies existence

L'More as binary of sames' differences
L'More is me being sexed in his private anal eye gaze

and I am L'More's negation
un humanly human

set up as meaningless
creating havoc's withdrawl of reality's volition of unnaturalness and queer

XXVI. Lick

L'More pollutes me alien rhizomatic
a pilgrim of panic ejection of exploded excrement in his private stall

I am a suspect under duress
L'More and normalcy failed me

history's flop L'More
I am sexuality's reject L'More

your buttfuck assassin L'More
concealed fictions L'More

punished L'More
your safe word illusion L'More

my heteronormative tormenter
fragmenting me un institutional

antistructural
un linear

I am an errant of complexity minus your other abstraction
feels having earned your quandary

XXVII. Plunk

My daily pilgrimage home
you'd find me L'More with no pleasure of being fucked with a Ziplock bag

but with threats of violence
with your torn off testicles in my mouth

my queerness' pilgrimage of terror's topography
where I become revealed through your repressions' hegemony on the Orange County streets

you have me as relocation's positioning for I'm a peasant rose
authority's upset

charity's tulip vestment of perversities
my rectum your threat

an invert of possibilities
and other ways of inhabiting

I am torn up and used in my position
inverted L'More time space boundaries

un inhabiting this world
creating a divide but now in my Poetics!

XXVIII. Smash

L'More decides what comes into view and what orientates me
queer'd latitude and longitude on the margins

L'More's repressive problemize'd playbook
if he'd allow me to enter his infernal anal halo of rhizomatic possibilities

and will to his rectal knowledge my performance is vengeance on this nation
my disclosure of offenses against nature staging a dream of self realization

trying to keep me in my institutionalized place of evil's effeminacy as I fuck your hole
Kant's *Categorical Imperative* a compulsive repetitious aggression to prevent my penetration

I am your AIDS cult
sweetened cum drinker

a social disease
THE END OF AMERICA

save the children queerness' future stops here defect
L'More is a taxonomist interloper in my opposition

let us journey L'More
not as Dante's guard of Virgil but as an abject memory

an agent
held caprice'd by language

by self
by other

by bad faith's confessional symptomatic urgent interchange poetic emergency
imagining your way out

claiming the world you want to enter L'More
wide legged splayed lubed up ready for my fucking stick

hedonism's healing haiku
reparative reading possibilities

L'More and me naked and wet before the gasses
bent and jacking off in this rhizomatic oven

as this body sun sets my own evil secret guiding me like lethal sugar
L'More is killing me as I kill SELF

this performance un'ushered
this queer theater unseated

XXIX. Sock

is he an angel at the golden gates of my performance
it is midnight in my Tolstoy

L'More's inherited parental education
what did your family teach you about your anus

why did they not learn you the pleasures of buggery
your criminal hole's jury not lawed

I'm crimes offspring and your cadaver violator
I fucked and toured your mothers corpse L'More

your father's sunshine
I fucked it L'More

I'm counter nature
L'More my judge my jury my executioner

oppositional self degenerescences' management of me
and my disturbance eliminator is out your sphincter

your private
my public

L'More's exposed anal hole
televised to the sun

corrective discourses
and onanistic traps

XXX. Bash

Ode to you
L'More's anus erasure

Oh l'amour
Broke my heart

Now I'm aching for you
Mon amour .

What's a boy in love
Supposed to do?

Regimes of penetration deposed
L'More's mechanism repress his own desires

and strictly projected segregation to reduce his forbidden desires
my non conjugal anus reject a front to your panic

a stalwart will closed down
consciousness bullied out of me

out of sight L'More
I AM NEEDED

like a disappearing haram denied my queerness of joyful criminal pleasure
persecuted and an inquisition of my anus

pushing back into private
what you've made public

in your othering of me
and my bad faith horrified at the flower of my secret

forcing my pleasure priest
confessional

XXXI. Whop

he is dust
he is mint

geranium's wuss othering and queering
this anal performative proscenium

L'More was all sternness and buttons to the neck
turtlenecked pharmakon

fuck L'More's hole
a remedy

fuck L'More's hole
a poison

fuck L'More's hole
a scapegoat

fuck L'More's hole
my moral agent other

XXXII. Uppercut

L'More stripping me of my national identity of my humanness for his sick survival
a piece of disposable plastic

a funerary for subjectivity
poetics infected refugee in L'More's nation

no right to rights
what lays inside is expulsion as I thread the hole

L'More's private is my public
Lynched and scorched

L'More's hole explosion
my public execution

my queer leisure exposed crossing the threshold
L'More violates me in his penal colony

excludes me
banishes me

make me pilgrim's stranger
this queer's procreation fraud of rectum's nerves and vapors

and the phantasmagorical phenomena of my possession
L'More is my faggotry in my cells

it is pedagogy
a religion cult

medicinal faggotry
purged surgically

removed by heteronormative procreation
mutation's derivation infirmed pathological

a perversion
in my exuberant debaucherous excesses

XXXIII. Pummeled

L'More my cure
shut your anus for I'm a disease that ends humanity

a burden of abnormality's hermaphrodite phthisic erythorbic depletion of lineage
pervert's sterility of the future un nurtured and exiled

I am your occupation originator of the non law
L'More you subjugate as self preservation and I dismantle your anus

for you to protect your bloodline from this diseased faggot
in heredity's suburbia

XXXIV.Whammy

but what of your dreams L'More
anal imposter

seizes hold of life in order to suppress
submit or be destroyed

L'More's anus
up in flames

to protect from biological danger
to safeguard society and to disallow this life

I AM THE END OF BIOLOGY
poetics guillotined on the threshing floor of Homocaust's rhizomatic citadel

flinched your sphincter exiled tight in internal expulsion and exclusion
with redrawn boundaries un belonging

queer rehab reify and recenter
performance exhaustion

faggotry is near life and not a real life
this discomfiting body obsolete in your revulsion

and its dissolute pleasures bore desire'ight out of you
I'm a kike faggot riding your hole into agencies while fertilizing our grammar with garbage

XXXV. Swipe

L'More's hole
Go artifice!

Go unnatural latch!
Go heaven the way of buggery!

Go un rubbered tip in your sweet ass L'More and let me eat at it!
Go other!

Go language!
Go poetics!

Go deep!
Go moans!

Go pleasure!
Open up L'More!

Go empathy!
Go dragon!

Go hard and pleasure roll it in your fig
for the world will reveal itself as you twitch and punch me rhizomatic

XXXVI. Bonk

name your victims
for you will sell a blueprint for disintegrates

and assume *the patinas of dusty chthonic wisdoms*
erasures could not serve better authenticities

turning your anal ashes
into poetic prose Twombly

when a mountain doesn't listen
say a prayer to the sea

the sea salt drink of nightmares
and your chubby lil' fingers bury your brethren

turning your cock into blossoms
for I will not know my narrative without L'More

he knows my story
it's in every follicle of his asshole

XXXVII. Swat

turtlenecks' stranglers dent my own way in need of charmed audacity's
natures sway

pigs at the trough
pigs at the trough at the absence of god

L'More rescue me
everyone's implicated and EDUCATION IS DEAD

Go judgement!
court this queer

I'm a coffin seller
and a funeral crier

I can draw a crowd
your anal voyeur

wearing out the mirror
a broker of death

without permission's worth I am your kids who'll never be born
my chalked murder outlines rainbow pink

L'MORE WHEN YOU LET ME FUCK YOU
I WILL BECOME AN AMERICAN

your wilted flower delivered is my rape
and my true life is not your ersatz demoralized memorial

I am
islet

XXXVIII. Collision

was L'More ever a baby taught to feel
will he get a death certificate for solitary's grave in my fecundity's scars

my body this locker room humiliated shirts versus skins
a pilgrim's cells of hopeful rhizomatic performance liberation

XXXIX. Slog

what would James Baldwin do L'More

L'More designed me a homophobic contraption or an extravagant pageant

James Baldwin would write you off the avalanche pedestal
but under your penis shadow I do not have the guns to ask for healing

can I ever be brave
James

XL. Zinger

I live on a planet that made bread ice cream and imagined unicorns
yet you death me horizontal vertically

I am rows of engineered corn
I am a plant

a pyramid made of steel
a rainbow revolution!

I've learned from my death that you hate my altruism L'More
I'm oxygen in you a loaded black gun bird

put in the crisper and edited
this rhizomatic rage rainbow

change'd me chemically
to resist you L'More

I am *a brave new world*
I am *passions slave's* slave

I am an edit before death
that longevity forgives in my own and other words

XLI. Knock

language I am a flying green beetle or a roach
I don't want the edit

I reject your genetic modification
your sphincter fear repels me

unmapped an outsider in the inside a giant sphincter of fear
I am a fly storm of maggots crucified on your wood

I am fuck you L'More
I will kill you for your hole and your protection is an invisible cloak

I will out you
like a 1980's bad faggot joke cloistered in closet AIDS outings

XLII. Spank

L'More's anus cult permeates this United States of America
as you worship the anus god in your private stall

my application
denied

your cock in my anus doesn't define me L'More does it
as I litigate your anus hate in my rhizomatic court

L'More wanted the filthy boys that lived across Cathy Street to stick their fingers in his butt
instead of mine

inauguration in your anus
my disinfectant

for your children and the nation
I have made them up into a little bundle of sticks

a Christmas faggot to feed the fires in the winter palace of your King
L'More

am I in your way
I exist outside queer

how many things will L'More turn his back
I turn my back on L'More bent over

always public your lacerations
landing on my fecundity scabs

XLIII. Pugilist

concentricity's consent
I could have been your murderer L'More but I chose rhizomatic poetics

the tears you have for no one would sear your face
homophobia ages you like dried out Indian flower garland's

a necromancer written in your micro aggression handbook
L'More you are cruelty without beauty

aesthetics' wounded bird
a mother boy

a filth mechanic
virus engineer my tormentor

shave off a part of yourself
until nothing is left

but your torn off testicles in my hand
L'More a saboteur

like handing you a loaded shot gun of other
L'More guns for my performance

your addiction to my hell within me
threatening the balance of our cravings

XLIV. Burn

I am faggot without future
L'More there is money all over your shit hole and I want to lick it

deliverance's atonement walk over my corpse and bankrupt me'queer
I am going to stick my head in the oven and it will be your fault

those that happen to forget
I am dying my family

for I am derelict in L'More's sterilization of me
a sewn up rhizomatic sphincter sold on the free market

you smell of dry crusty rectum
L'More is a butcher leading other slaughter

marl hole's filthy birds shower from the Venus demon
and feast your eyes on my ugliness

for I won't be weeping with a remedy abhorring this persona
coma in your committee for you are denied my bread

fuck boys from the Sturmabteilung unit have arrived
for god's arrival and for immediate witnessing

this queer leper filled with piss
drown on the pyre

worthlessness I am off to the vault to steel the cure as refusals' reject
a frother my virus' honey

yes mother
today's lesson

L'More
homophobic rage drowning in piss

as Mustafa reject
nausea's artist

when I pull L'More's trousers down
what do I see digesting in sodomic' castration

L'More grab your pad and pencil
and sketch these dimensions

boss man release
roaches in my anus as production of me

hearts conscious absence suffocated in my crib dragging you out the closet door
never a refugee with my identity wrapped up in your interpretations

the nation's plague manager cap my slits' claim of destined misfortune's fortunetude
your occupying patriarchal expose discrediting yourself and misrecognition me

L'More in libido's narcissism
sewn ass regime discipline's disciples of state law

your otherness seeking to commodify my problematized disorder
carry your hate crime written upon your anus cheeks marked for death

disjointed in sovereignty's complication
ritualized performances in my criminalized zone of abandonment

my innumerable confined disavowed means of scope
excluded ascensions punitive with fatigued L'More

your conforming hole
vasectomized and a refuge'd of others *homomascunationsocialitity*

my gazed essence misrecognized as other
written down as a system of difference

war armaments against parasitic rhizomatic poetics
L'More undo me concluded in your codified identity

employing jurisdiction on this public anal pleasure
and bold bow forward variances

collapse your rectum to the sun
loosen sphincter control L'More

this text written in and on your anus
your pleasures' sodomy emancipations' in my queer possibilities un male your eye L'More

yield demand's rhizomatic mirrors to expose your hole revealed
and heartened in certain clandestine cords to self revelations

un instituting dispair's rivalry
eluded and exclude

in the scorn of collective determinants
L'More your bourgeois restless intransigence escapes invention

your estrangement in an ankle grab
so I may arrive at your police'd confusion

released of terroristic authoritarian contrivances in your woman's spread
L'More's phallocentric fixation

an indeterminate incarceration
a dogma's bitch assassin of paradise

regulators of my parsimony yield your fleapit to pleasure's sovereignty
L'More's law de erection agent

the authority of progenitors testicles in hand
occupied and anatomized with fusses anxieties

signifier's fragmented mutilated privation in this locus' famine
imperialistically negating cock indulgence in my desideratum

fiction engine this fantasy pageant
queer paranoia

amputate me
dismember me

castrate me
cannibalize me

decapitate me
rape me

other me
dequeer me

terrorize me
spit on me

public me
instrument me

surveil me
pleasure me

fuck me

dominate me

perform me

alienate me

justify me

bludgeon me

bugger me

lynch me

gun me

knife me

bomb me

poison me

fictionalize me

electrocute me

gas me

drown me

absorb me

punch me

tie me

strangle me

run over me

x ray me

burn me
trap me

penetrate me
misrecognize me

lose me
outrage me

brutalize me
mandate me

bribe me
abscond me

subordinate me
objectify me

master me
purify me

boss me
fracture me

judge me
void me

avoid
me

internalize me
trap me

exchange
me

sell me
strike me

mutilate me
suicide me

fire me
burn me up in flames

autocide medicide murder suicide self immolation avunculicide familicide filicide fratricide geronticide honor killing infanticide matricide neonaticide nepoticide parricide patricide pedicide prolicide senicide siblicide sororicide uxoricide amicicide androcide assassination capital punishment casualty collateral damage democide populicide ecocide extrajudicial killing euthanasia familiaricide femicide gynecide gynaecide gynocide feticide gendercide genocide
homicide justifiable homicide human sacrifice massacre murder manslaughter omnicide targeted killing extrajudicial killing xenocide deicide episcopicide regicide tyrannicidealgaecide acaricide avicide biocide fungicidegermicide herbicide insecticide larvicide microbicide miticide nemacide parasiticide pediculicide pesticide scabicide spermicide teniacide theriocide vermicide virucide vulpicide famacide linguicide urbicide FAGGOCIDE

XLV. Flame

FAGGOT

XLVI. Torture

America's revulsion spans the abyss of delegitimates' contagion
this abasement'd possession

my abject pleasure is a humiliation decree
un historied

L'More organ's lackluster cult oriented in suppositions' reinforcement
anchored estranging distinctiveness sodomitically unmans me

L'More specter containing
each other from your rectal discerning penetration

fears baked to take
cut of my lance and wear it whole Hester albatross'd

inside my broadcasted un fix'd shadow errant queerhood
unearthed in others yielded in performance abandonment

and my intwined histories of indefinite differentiation
this annihilations' statue

stigma story
a telling statute

allegiance regime's unexpected archivist
a reproduction reject

I was promised at my birth rape a rose's garden
and all I got was pricked

I'm un ween'd futurities coffin of nails' empty vessel statue
a fictive law reflecting social rupture

an aborted queer
L'More clings to the thigh of identity like a homesick abortion

epistemological regime's

mortal coil

XLVII. Battle

I want to thank the people
that helped me get here

L'More
Fred Phelps

Jesse Helms Ron DeSantis
your filthy holes' jouissance

antagonistic lucidity
where I reside in your residue

lubed up L'More and my palpated chubby finger rings and pokes
rings and pokes your phenomenological expulsion

an un propitious theatre oriented at your phantom table set
as I eat your pigsty in a kitchen of one's own malady disoriented

my other inhabits your pleasure space
locked behind your bathroom bolted egress

XLVIII. Fracas

L'More ask me to sit for your painting chronicling the unfamiliar homing
as my homo'ing device emerges in this rhizomatic stick fire'd faggot pilgrim HOMOCAUST

and I sit for no one now
always arriving poetic

not a pupil of god's will but errant
L'More an ornery geld

factions obligatory plea against the noxious bigotry of the govern'd other world
with futurity passing defenses of diseased

self
not self's virile prophesizing a bourgeois parable

your dick L'More
sword of middle class preservation

subject to other corrective valetudinous compliant
perverse bud of man taking consort as liege

THIS HOMOCAUST BODY NATION
A DYNASTY IN CRISIS

XLIX. Broil

L'More the anxious man sum
anitsodomatical procreator

unruptured
inlet

safe from effeminacy's mollie trapper
my repudiation

something authoritatively dangerously warm came up L'More's silent orifice
L'More's masculine body penetrated

imposed depravity's propriety usurped my language
a domineering significance bending me other and over'gain

composing inferiority
misappropriating my pain body's abject constitutional evacuation of excrement

inverted this performance in fits of abject vomit
cast out as I cum drink his solipsistic assault on logic's nature

interlocked his anal eye stare a ruckus in proper jurisdiction
shoved down his bourgeois throat

goes the nation
un capitol'd decapitation

un seat your essentialist dirt frame
your besieged anus state goes the law

govern my edifying confines
terminating this queer taint

this hystericization error
a public emblem queer

legitimate in sodomy's private secretions I rise

my un humdrum'd poetic collapse shoved down his gangling milky throat

L. Beat

I am AIDS framed
squashed cabbage draggletailed guttersnipe pygmalionite

L'More hoisted hoodwinked perverted instrument
an anus virtuoso

I am denaturalized
a transposal involution

this academia
a sodomite

this rhizome
a sodomite

sodomy's illegitimate embryonic poetic logos
dismantled maenad in Orpheusian massacres

I am your twisted Mapplethorpe'd whip shoved up your anus
I am the NEH Four rammed down your throats

Tim Miller
Holly Hughes

Karen Finley
John Fleck up in flames

my front
crammed down your back

with voyeuristic obscurity
in queer civic defense

LI. Death

Evacuate your anus L'More
emptied and impregnate us unrestricted with disconcerting intimacy

as I quench your contaminated fluids and retch'd latency
disavowed hoarded face cum full of fiction frenetic fantasy and dramatization

L'More's masculinity a sage on the stage
an anus of one's own

life's but a walking shadow L'More
a poor player that struts his anus and frets his penetration upon the heteronormative stage

and then is heard
no more

L'More
It is a tale told by a fucking idiot in need of love

full of screams sound and fury
signifying other

phallic's clout in my nationalized identity
western civilization

anus fucked liberation
castrated *out out* with balls in hand

the collapsed of poetic apex in this gays' gaze merriment
wretches vile in this licentious Homocaust Queerdom

pelted transgressive sodomites evaded pleasure from behind
hind sight blind mobius loops transverse immovable locuses anal'ized

you are Christ L'More
Jesus' non queer

not sexed
not fucked

no sunshine raying out your anus
not a rhizome

father son and the holy queer
a poetic invert

Oh L'Amour
Oh poesy's remind

I am a living hate crime
and Jesus is a sodomite!

Rhizomatic Pilgrim

exultant marrow narrows liberty
decries bindles on fugitive deleterious shores

tasting the night of day
more naked in alarm

abducting the world of hunters
another history already a runaway

on the trails of deerhounds
the bamboo shoots mo'ment

their corroded nudities muscle'd root in the space of the world
we grow faster than our verses can chance

.

Saturn moon found itself large in extasy's militant unity
the Sequoia shades the message of the catkins carrying contemptable jungles

our absent landscapes
un evaluative solitude

decorated by the blood of loss
planting a delible scar

endlessly un root the soil

mute emerges a lesson of attached selves

the taciturn receptacle versus your mounts subsists

fell drunk amid skirmish

contaminant horizon

incomplete drama of necessity

a vocation mired tragedist'quotidian fastened to succulence

the rusted sow of other

avatar of possibilities

pandemonium space of absolutes

hullabaloo of tripwires
and echoes of torment

new languages from languages
spectacle and tussle desiccated

quiet noise opacity
collect floods that not rain

move towards fertilizing
the moons of our loins

tide noise deaf
opacity runs venerating you

land which gawks the twilight sacrificing nudity in a state of arthritic abscesses
amongst my shallowing arteries

limpidness thick where I drench

populating discourtesies dialectic harrows your harvest

amputate walking refusals hunted by artifice
arid mirrors rush at orts meat

icy an offal of rat touched loin
travel onerous conduits between languages

no intention resists the upsurge fantasy
illumination becomes stellated

fugitive triumphant escapes
writing the shadow of what will write

convict of parenthesis aspiring to live all my births

avatar of the we who says I with me

196

plasma earth amalgamated cleanse'd in the molten tuff
the lair choked absent cadavers

essence'd bodies hemmed in the depths grew their vehement
rot the rock

derision sings its tango
pass through bodies unemployed

exalted secret liberty
no community here

be stripped of its individualities extracted against this drive
dead scorched in the forgotten earth of our voices

return deprived bellow before innumerable waves' enemies

appease feverish yesterday to weave distant becoming

199

phenomenal denials of histories
revealing me to myself

our conscious germ tool's the weapon
untangle the web the world catches us in

absence beating in the cry

disgorge the song

thirsty toes in mire the night rose abridged in the inconsequential subjugations

otherness fortified us

lair of evils breath acerbic
humans lime'd

depths begins lack
remains a stranger

ends contaminated
every nations' yesterdays

jar'd directionless
traumatisms successions

elocutionary synergy liason'd
to the totality world

language languages' dearth
the vagabondage poetics' elocutionary mass

gaze of both sides projected onto self
only total eyes other's either

what glitters and moves immovably
a simplified universe

the most intense coppice
the sky of the page

clipped the midnight eludes
erecting language out rock deserted history dissipated smothered misery

vomiting un learnt poetasters
abandon fervor elsewhere

bricking a poem
in my language to understand you

extract a basilica from mucks' avowals solitary transgressions

who prompts abandonment abjuration assailing

chasm'ous indecision while renaissances the laborer dialectic scouts
chambering an open self

imposing immobile abyss'in the disunity vocations of unity
capsize'd in jolting derisory

en route to a new communal order
of equals' sacred network

touch your hands
I will show my scars or something else

protecting
this soil

until self and crowd out fiery performance
why not be more than faggot under the authority of fathers

surveillance

I was grey to marry me

map lines language
the pilgrim crime untraced

float concrete narratives
next to each

this city satire
fragility's rise in concentricity

books we hadn't read
this book pilgrimage still to be read

what has the land seen
mule trains

a small temple
symbolically castrating itself

those with no one left
remember them

spasms of genocide blisters their muscle pain
torn closets and cabarets at the stations of the cross

a right to assert empire on its empire

the pathology of survivors

a dead donkey twitching in the street
sleeping eternal in cow piss

cerulean sounds the burial sky
coal rot of Joshua's miasma

gang mourning green damning the torpid
a farewell to understanding

my recent departures
domesticated sounds a'knowing

this lone poetic pilgrimage'd
heir oblique

human hoarfrost this harvest

sun lucidity

its literaturates

corporeal armaments in the vaults of this Homocaust museum

high cliffs inside you dawn the rock

the treasure of low vicissitudes

push some islet against the wall

my lingering eye illumes the Icarus depths

this past
is plunge

chaos directives
afore the other

dazzling in the frolics'
successive directions

the ethnologist shelf

born in my exhaustion

vertiginous clarities

poetic signs of my experiences opposites to the other

the pilgrim massif its homonym
inventors of the quiver

drunken ascension unsnarl'd canna meanders
the inestimable thatches of dearth

expanse pilots of panes of blood

left on the sidelines of this Homocaust crime

spume my watches
bankrupt in its gloom

to bestow at last to close
the only splendor of its word illuminating

this degeneration I must prevaricate
finally touching my winter

symmetry of plantings hinders me
submitting to an unfounded order

abutting a catalogue of fixed forms affectation or coquetry
lips of the earth

a handkerchief atop a wind

gnaws devoted

a turf of spikes

latescence perdition in mute desire of the strange nuptials of dust

chapped limbs of remembrance
your drupes spasm in tender milk

ooze a prune tree in my manuscript of hindrances

flowering dirt

fructify blooming muds

ascend fades the bumps of bleed

229

femora captive in a roused monster
chorus encumbrance

my margins retreat the anew
rototiller blades these pangs of blood

the denuded dirts

star ire bonce opaque bivouacs

hoarsened the cradles rime

dusky infrastructures at the summons of other moon moons

rigidity unpeopled

nascently whetted moves us outside self

not a stranger

errantry raises the voice of the impossible consults with the universe

chimera leave courage at chaos
mangle'd blenches

vex the nail of astrophysical recipes to the sedate ingress noosphere
a new'fangled providence

doused suns sepulchers' racket
houngans my wakening

mongrel draggings and cages
errancies elder my marrow calculated amongst the coal

vocative gluts grandiose pelt a ruddy employ
perennial naves the sows of tresses

branches pull the fertile dug
the end of fear is beauty

gangrene diamond the order of rag

hangs a hoarfrost pilfering echoes

tenebrate'd caresses an embargo'd word and enlivens the frigid

obliged in the renaissance of human episteme

rapture spatters the delta consecrated in gravity's vacancies

thrushing words' plentitudes in sand

kali yuga vapors

fugitive wick'd brine in the cerulean exit

clouds rain clouds

fields your eyes

catastrophic clasps the faults

the pillager of hulks have absconded their blood

this ember aggrieve'd statues agony of their cells

illume'armada fowl

certainty mends expanse

course swept my snow

discoveries

subtract myself

drought in purpose
muddling taxiderm'ily

executions by mortar'd proboscises
razzias interminable putrefaction

masticating nails elucidate the fabric of racket
I have branded many facades of acquiescence

secretion cart

the long gone solar system

in the odor of pebble

heraldic cognizance's arise

pilgrim no longer in my personages

a single frame ordained its unmeasure'd body

primordial world a reflexive reap
other expatriated self

nourishing reminiscence of unanimity of strangers
togethers'together

tangled parapets sneer mutilated arsenals against collective catastrophes
transmit effervesces' perplex

denials' denial perambulator

fuss lost in the bee nest

slurs of earth that buttress poesy

deracinates my appetite

macerates my invention

we are adolescence in my birth'd possesses

euphoria book tenders

and the poet scans their sagas

clear song of my many births

malediction my imbroglio flees in the dance of echoes and arrest it

glimmers refracted in my dual state blasted against contexts limit'd actualities
the frail fixities of search

249

Narcissus bends into his glass'd air

a syntax of melancholias in a temple of sigh

dialectical triumphs
imbued in reflected unicity

a sorrow coat of cracked pain deposits
ugliness and go

hello clementine a métier palaver
feel more with less

crude a sizzling sky

recourse deceits outwit drab sulk in igniting potency

fluxes of sap molten
densify the surly word

gravitating in poverty
words jacket me emblematically'umbilical

being wants to move penetratingly in escapes

stagnant in the occupied of erratic fitting privations of my solitude

there outside met arrivals a good many deviations
confronting your own landscape

suffering unimaginable light
the rupture'd consenting to settings

the jade stem far from its man bosoms be your call to army
language'd pastoral lurks flamboyant

disquiet feeds glimpse the day

subterfuge residues fixed pacifications in the cum of exigency

our sheathings the tender lime'd kin alterity the dandelions of history

so many a trial

all that pilgrim are found

the people of the verb in the exalted kip of glisten

tang the harvest gleaners to the shrines excretions
the ocher skins of the quasi

requiems of renunciations

requiems of our conveniences

relish dithering things

without conducting narratives for our conveniences

pilgrims' progress razzias
ends bliss in the swarming

my removed feet cricking immovably conceits hues the apple
time'd grey between the spring autumn'ing leaves

new coinage of this drunken boat canary'd anode of the lay

the poet pool'd errant

tussles in the echo

aggravate in the trenches

rustling the gents harmony in fissures

the verges of'transhumance

with the clay tossed afore your rung columns a reach
the poet revivifies their oath

elucidate torments ossuary
the discernment aurora of fonts

the dead time inked in the tattoos of gamble converted and hooked to the tilt
an exercise of echoes in the art of nomads

exigencies deaf intransigent voyages

germinate the dreamers subjectivity condescensions' collisions

265

it was in the lint in the laundry
between my vulva cracks

a ghost gone did it wrong

bivouacked in the middle of the Filchner-Ronne Ice Shelf

fig pecker
a slurry

primogeniture similitude robustesse in displeasure'd watch
etched in the ransack of modes between new and old potencies

unearthing
unearthings

twixt two secret'd others

gluts deracinated equivocations in the basin of suspension

contemplative not let go its game

on the thresholds of the dateless banks

magus gash'd encyclicals

blue bearded at the acme

moonfish convalescence against the movement of histories

a genocidal opera wishing I cosmos and grass

to profit one's euphoric liberty the lapidary orgasms of gushes
more dead than bayonetted vibrates

272

dues in light valorize combustion to desecrate the de naturer

the vibrant language of its boom

womb the sperm to this ether
spray the logic of marshalled assets

the mass of birth
all entirety

decerebrated peoples arm stretched to the realm of denials

the overseas judder of onetime

275

the rhythm frisk
maladies of enunciated tongues

inserted in maximum secret of our stupefactions
of our chaotic births

ever be warbled
a beleaguered cosmic estate

intervenes the bellicose lasso
vibrations of the othersphere

insouciant failure molt'd less'd the verdure trembles
the layer of nightfall in which to drown

desert pulp the meticulous sun
calculated calcine'd erosions festering on totems

thirsts historicity in the salvaged fate

metallurgists of old tales

relics of red earth

bones born hard to modish mod festoons

memory glebes'accident

contrabands' posterns of barbarism

initiative debuts

being the continue of tremble unsteady remains

contaminated apparatuses of conquest

trapped in the unsteadiness of contagion

reticent mutterings

the infamy of extirpation scour the hue of humus

glorioles the rose cell

nocturnal in the guano

rise absent seep

free of falses

every islet underwrites harmony
each ocean kiss a reticent cry out mouth'd at the abyss

Gehenna the mud demons
deport me to a novel of dirts

to suffer un landscape'd efforts

yesterday I reconquer planting one's pyramid renaissance'd in new meanings

287

the land quitted
ravaged by transports interred in the agony of the 'ntrapture'd

capitals an apt knife
un cuts the umbilical

but to carry perdition ceaselessly shelved
unmitigated in the advent rupture of optimism

sung raw in the melee of organic secreted momentum
denied dead in my echo lamented

the refrain of land neglected between two wicks of three lit
anonymous in the revere of palms at history end

amputated by bygones
we shallow from the past labrynth'ian sap flush with teeth

infinitesimal hell
troughs and pulpy parasites

spiral of mosquito stung catastrophes

gutter unalterable passerine hangars in the ghouls of lucidity

gullied muds

waiting in ignoble solitary navigations

grips not a solitary gleam

taxidermizing to root a total ungod'd

lattice walk
finding no shrines

un sung land judiciously stolen

histories not fitting us a rock not met

do not

water the rocks

bleed pages splinter'd in heart cinders
the vanity of this vamp

dermis memory

indissociable pulp pulps before a futile spark

solstices a pure kiss kiss on the mouths of the dead

opt'd for the wet'd sun

ripened bitter myrtle blazon body
a funerary rose rose

curvature of the earth
joist flanks the soil soils

our hands cry out the redolent clandestine
in the spittle of other

envision options disemboweled sand spells
all has not been explored

soundless throngs

closet remotest gone

wily pseudonyms indiscernible

we are no more I abetted yet stir'd and multiplied

cordyceps poetic de'grasp
teacher touch impending

thrown through the through window
surveying realms yet to come

various form'd matter deterritorialized
exteriority rupturesa *body without organs*

assemblage'd intensities map'd the world tree
the degrees of something else

language insulates

two steps back'd to nature

manufacturers diminution in the laws of creation
radical chaos'mos stymied conquest collapse ramified on the surface semiosis chains

ceaselessly memetic slangs slings multiplicities weave
proliferating line maps without trace

rings rupture
flat in poetic cum

charming the orchid bee

the bee apt the potting d'territorializing explodes

transversal semi state
not induce a vine grape

pewter horizons the devil's micturate

weed extends territory

decalcomania perfume'd without sameness

constructs map'd performic in the conflict of accurate

always map not a trace
un neutralize'd in the margins

not the parent bed
outgrowth'd the dualisms

rigidified universals blast accretions from their root assemblages

desire burgeoning

perverse hegemony tired of trees

probabilistic morph folly in the neuroglia arborescence

re rupture medusas' capture tree

phallocentric intrusions map'd auto'finite a'gone

waves of imagination

imaginal yoga un'undo

in construction of collapse

deform'd in battalions of sign

swum in the anti gene
a centered un becomings

plateaus interphenomena
poetry furniture in the re arrange

narcissisms in the bilbos of flight

convergent circles only for laughs self vibrating semiotic glows nomadologically unplugged

handsomely monster'd in rupture

un foundatedly nullify the ends

away go the river edges

reductive jeopardizes all

the thought purge of castration

ether deliriums

we storms of bees

frame without tissues cry not a dead body

infinitely dance

sucker for glitter against the gang of fixity

unreduced to a god non'decomposable intensities in the field of entangled

322

expeditions dance in the flight line

paranoid becomings in nuptial bodies

collective agents

naked in the mouth

non individual dromedaries

fox in throats of the language dirt

nomadic organs
un'body'd uncaptured ether

god judgement in the strata bands
schist comets in the un hum drum'd

structure binary understands'gone
breaking the sings of glories

dialogue medusas un tongue'd

sport in the rhizosphere

rhythms non totality rupturing histories

detached breaks no longer traditions' tangles

monuments un fixed in space

unboundary'd the dominant core nonhierarchical liberations

evolutive teleological curves

repugnant movements of consciousness in the time of your own think break sovereignty in new narratives

synchrony unbound

laws of desire

not single form in the pirate utopias' imaginal tribunals

dual order is redundancy mistress

imposing semiotic coordinates in the other words

languages obeys in my pretend agree
provocation in my negate

word work shovels at meaning pickaxe
your grammar a power marker to other

command order in language not life
saying for saying

indirect discourses metaphor me

mapped performative this faggot

performativesphere code nondeterminative
pragmatics shifters of the other elocutes in statement acts

this moment
redundancy in schisms time

accretions' mask
no individua in the dominance enunciations

referentially self'resonance in reason un sounded

there is no individua

assemblages collected pilgrim

discourse shifts in the transformation of bodies' strange

this speech act inserted here

rhizomatically instantaneous

you are a lone child language act
trapped Wittgensteinally fly bottle'd

341

history word order

hegemony's lover

swiping a certain sound is a horse and a bird
look at the circle stealing pictures

variable in'corporeal assemblages rupture rupture regimes
tongues speak in speak

344

xenoglossic fruitage

effectuate possibilities with tongue'd autobahn speed

totals de limited

re animating the sacralized unconstraints

carry the threshold bride'd over

purged dis metanarratives reproach'd in reject

scribe to have no body

vacate injustices

undo credential edicts

no demands persisting the same

rid our selves tradition slaves

drive out universal devils

eunuch's punch bowl discursive nodes

plateaus discursive imagines

disturbed suspense

stars above Neptune in the rhizo branch

proceed in un certainty

under the infinite continuity

denounce the never accept outside the unities

free from the construct theory'irium

pose a question of clutter

reformed events in the invisible why's collide

you are running out of pages to burn
living a humbled life

sorry old
under this education is not a good small

live into their own
always thinking of others' good

but no one said hello
to end up useless living in a mess

go before it gets too hot
you are running out of pages to burn

all the devils in my desk drawer earned this earth

it's so easy to write this poem for you

poet'eve the boat no belly

floats the human condition

concrete to rhizome
virgin river in the valley of fire

plant talking
the other house of way

advise and direct
the refugia refugium

nunatak land above glacier field
archaic arctic disjunct in the evolutionary arms race

roots and wings glacial erratic

do not turn your back on the tide

gilded

I am San Francisco working from a word phrase bank

coveted veered in lethal sugar

my problems beautiful like Boulder chinook

sending signals

talking to each other'motherkids

mycelium a pilgrim spores

gene carrying systems

synesthesia

poetics

haecceity jazz

a pilgrim community of strangers

wrestled with the d'sweated virus an un snow crush'd dogma
scattershot abstruse

thrown in free association
migrates indebtedness to disorder possibilities in turn

frenzied neologisms a self referential toss off
poesy designs its tongues

Rhizomatic Pilgrim: Discursive Youth

reechoed in my urine soaked sheets
as I thought the lights flying by my window shade were UFO's

for in the 1970's that was a thing on TV and in movies
Greys probed in the third kind

and where the neighboring Humdinger dive bar
pilots drank from the nearby base next to the Stop-n-Go where I stole Butterfingers

cinnamon sticks and candied cigarettes
here nuclear weapons aimed eastwest on seal beaches

where I washed in the blood of the lamb and swam in rat pools
amongst the world's stench under Reagan uncomforted AIDS quilt

when everything is taint in your infancy you need the gods to come down and crack

for it all goes missing on the back of milk cartons

forever

this fag

we always feared killer bees

UFO's

nuclear bombs

men in vans and serial freeway killers

during Hebrew lessons in somber song
where I would swoon on lethal sugar highs

I sometimes sucked Berman's cock in front of the Torah in the synagogue
in front of God

Cypress had a Mervyns
a Del Taco

cows
strawberry crow'd fields

and no
James Baldwin

how can their house burn

when they love Jesus so much

371

the Homocaust
is in my heart

everything about me
has been used against me

at the Church of the Holy Phallus

a room was set aside for golden showers

and we buttfucked

hopefully

with AIDS on

periphery

horror
at home

horror
at school

horror
in me

sewn into my fashion on Valley View Blvd towards the 405 to Los Angeles
where faggots drip down Melrose

flaming Duran Duran crimps and old punks cock stare
in the toilets of the *Odyssey* or *Peanuts*

where Nina Hagen begs *New York New York*
and Kate Gardner Haysi Fantayzee *Shiney Shineys*

and Tin Tin kisses me
a cypress tree gun

was it suburb trick or treat
or was it an inauguration

I own the Hiroshima bomb

for I am American

I am a fly storm of maggots crucified on your cross
Ton Sur Ton crimped aqua'd net hair folded pant leg cuff

in the 70's
kids ruled the neighborhood

I wanted Daniel Day Lewis to cum in my mouth

when I repeatedly watched *The Unbearable Lightness of Being* or *My Beautiful Laundrette* meet me in the fragmented domiciles

and address this language of loss

if my family wrote love letters to me now
it would be too late

Eartha Kitt
Liz Fraser

Grace Jones
Madonna and Nina Hagen

became
my sisters

I would cum a little

when watching *Midnight Express*

everything
heterosexual

mattered
FUCK YOU AIDS

I was not allowed
to be worth it

I was born
with PTSD

my chalked murder outline
is rainbow and pink

fuck Ronald Reagan
he lined us up

shot us while we bled
rainbow

when will the pink American
just become American

in the uterus

had I had known this violence

I lived in glorified violence

but I tried to be Lola Beltran

CODA

rake the leaves inside this house
serial killers were once six years old like me

this is my home jail body
when are you going home out of my sight

this is my home where I carried the ruined city
under my skin

last caps of breathe this burden
a place of resistance

no boundaries
careful with my burden

again the Homocaust is in my heart

a farewell to understanding

Homocaust Pilgrimage

Namu-Myo-Ho-Ren-Ge-Kyo

"Civilization is not a matter of having electric lights, nor flying by airplanes, nor making atomic bombs. Civilization means not killing human beings, not destroying things, not waging war, but instead respecting each other. - Nipponzan Myohoji, the Most Venerable Nichidatsu Fujii.

Ultimately, we have just one moral duty: to reclaim large areas of peace in ourselves, more and more peace, and to reflect it toward others. And the more peace there is in us, the more peace there will also be in our troubled world. —— Etty Hillesum

The past is never dead. It's not even past- William Faulkner

Boulder

Colorado

Na-Mu-Myo-Ho-Ren-Ge-Kyo

Na-Mu-Myo-Ho-Ren-Ge-Kyo

I am beckoned from orange counties to walk embodied embroider'd steps

a discursive pathway to my renaissance

I do not hesitate a subversion in strip mall promises
this walk may befit a suburban Baldwin

this pilgrim interloper between divine and human worlds
take these queer legs beneath these jeans

where poesy has the right to assert its empire
in the dusty verdigrises of acumen

where erasures of Cypress California
forgotten here in this office of no office

raging in Boulder Chinook wind
and Jean Benet Ramsey ribbons

could not serve better authenticities turning my ashes into poetics
with these rainbow feet suitable for pilgrimage

let's fly this road christened pink like a cogito thaumaturgist phoenix toward the within
for we are gonna wear our compassions in the shade of Ginsberg

with my worn toe nails eventual peel beneath the fungus heft of my tormentors
ending timeworn memoirs

with how beautiful the world is lit in instances of muteness' brackish silo
as I learn in this office a stranger to the world

a proposal to befit my masters

I sublet my SELF

Prague
Czech Republic

everything into a poem
even the thump pounding disco under my room via Heathrow

you leave your empty passport
at the front desk so the polis know

you exist
here

there is a river view unlike the Mississippi
Vltava off the Mala Strana

Na-Mu-Myo-Ho-Ren-Ge-Kyo
somnambulistic mania

not American dreaming as Donna Summer fights
and wins *working hard for the money*

breaking through these medieval floors
or was it *love to love you baby* raying disco moans beneath my rock hard bed

Orange County California
is an escaped suburban hell fire

I became time's Bohemian infant staring at the medieval clock
strolling the gargoyle'd Charles Bridge and the mangled tombstone'd Jewish Ghetto

under Kafka's eye un roached
to St Vitus cathedral treasures and the Basilica of St George babushkas

to the alchemists' Golden Lane
then meet myself

Auschwitz is a non place
for Oswiecim Poland was renamed by Nazi's

I am up against history
and languages'invasions

Roma Rokker Nais Tuke caravan a wagon to peace
manufactured behind a red curtain

as apparitions float up
raging from these narrative tracks

Oswiecim
Poland

convocation Auschwitz
Na-Mu-Myo-Ho-Ren-Ge-Kyo

Auschwitz *I* concentration camp that has been driven into me since the rape of my birth
growing up son of Jacob now an atheist dustbin with children thrown away here

ghosts rent outside my room's window
near the *arbeit macht frei* violins' cry

this Homocaust kaddish
ode to burnt stick pilgrims

my Homocaust

decaying hands catching smoke on the selection of tracks

transforming blood space out of popsicle sticks and brass nuts
strings pulled from a stripped camp uniform marked pink or black triangle'd

candle wick a *nigun* accompanied by a flute and the mournful beat of monk drum and chant
in Auschwitz hangs the gallows

like a vertical coffin listening to their fate
poetry will free you

lyrical fervor
baked in this oven

Oswiencim is a city that continues anachronistic

near the gas'd shower nozzles as we pray prayers on the choosing platforms

amongst the collected dentures

yellow patches and pink triangles of Hitler's maenads and twin children experiments

climbing the piles of shaved heads and prosthetics

Nazi labeled emptied suitcases among dreams

grayed shoes and hair for mattresses and pillows

Auschwitz Birkenau now a museum

the end of the track

MEMORIAM AND GAZA

the children of Theresienstadt Ghetto
follow me

as I set off alone
at 4am jetlag to the crematorium with the healing dirts of Chamayo New Mexico I collected

I place these dirts at the oven shoot marked Volkswagon and Mercedes
where a real gas pilot flame still burns

in this gas oven
a ghost

we gather as pilgrims in convocation at Auschwitz rust'd death can
a walk in ashes

the coal Poland air that spits black resistance and renaissance
for the rope hanger branded pink

walk downtown meet the mayor of Oswiecim
only one Jew left living

drumming to a small church after a bridge called history's back
we are offered bread and salt

Japanese monks in their saffron robes
meet another Hiroshima

the towns' people live amongst the demented plan of extermination
near the selection platforms where ironic cellos play

symbolically
castrating themselves in this modernity

where the Stradivarian's played a requiem for a kind Roma woman
whom always gave people cigarettes in the mud under the Madonna moon

unclothed to her ending with no one left to remember
from the ones addicted to violence and once dead

the flames incircle in the filth
like faggots at the harrows

stick
collection

the scent of burnt flesh
excrement lingering

or
is that hope

I am the death to Auschwitz

this queer

or
am I a Rabbi

in my kaddish
pilgrim

toddler shoes
rubber nipples

Shoah sweaters and children thrown away
amongst the piles of false teeth and eye glasses

imaginings
up in flames

ONE BY ONE

not 6 million

and everyone danced
the hora

prosthetic Nazi

heart

suitcases confiscated from unsuspecting arrivals

Nazi's emptied a suitcase Weiss Goerg 12 8 1935 ah 606

a gold ring   423

tallis

eye glass instruments

spouse'd pictures

torah

horror

Poland sleeps in WWII museums
tragically between Stalin and FDR

awakes
muddled

PALESTINE

GAZA

Pszcyna

Czech Republic

step into Tanglefoot

the Duchy of Pless

in the spasms of genocide

blistered feet and muscle

phantom pain fragmented

extinct in urban gmina's hypnotic Nazi coat of arms

attacked by Hussites where later Jews settle

east of the river Oder

Bielsko Biala
Czech Republic

white remains south of the Duchy of Auschwitz and north of the house of Habsburg
sparsely settled steps

we are not *Einsatzgruppe*
bearing peace cranes not scepters as we eat at your salt bread and dance

Novy Jicin
Czech Republic

queer in this topography
universally ceremonious to hang in each geography

as reminiscences with their pilgrim's comfort
callers embraced in love and peace

un cliché'd
not as non communal strangers up in flames

Na-Mu-Myo-Ho-Ren-Ge-Kyo
Na-Mu-Myo-Ho-Ren-Ge-Kyo

Czech hospitality
this altruistic embodiment of jouissance

a fifty foot stretched knot wooden table
an abundant plot altogether for seventy two wearied empathies

with splendid sugar distortedly diverse in flour'd fashions
with not a speck of table to be seen underneath

snow flake Venice Burano Isle Italy filigree doily
tray'd artisanly performed

we delight eating
orange red Mazurek sunset flakiness

Dobosh torte
buttercreamed sponges

nut rolled and wheeled date night Kolaczki Tiffany diamond shaped
raspberry apricot affairs

bubble cake plums
plume bublanina s'blumami

seminola clafoutis
kifle kilfice od oroha crescents

powdered sugar shirt fallen smears
Russian Mexican wedding cookies married to perfection

Ciastka Kruche z Orzechami
floats fragile pecan

next to rose shaped Roszke Rosky as my grandma Rose made these little horns under her
bosom next to the Kiev sour pickle jar in Lakewood California

and Florentynki
seen in every Jewish bakery in New York City

with smeared candied orange
like bubbe's lipstickin her fake fur

Vanilkove Rohlicky
fallen hazel nut snow

Amareti
a traveler from the south

Ciasteczka Orzeszki walnut shaped
like a desserted chinese dumpling at a lazy Susan table in Xi'an amongst tera cotta warriors

Cukrovi Susenky
fruit filled shortbreads piled tall

Kaiserschmarrn royal
named after Franz Joseph I

apple pear berry'preserve
Makowiec a poppy Afghan visit

crostata
cherries berries apricot peaches

Kremes
puffed classiques

chiacchierre
Grappa crunch

Torrone
hazelnut pistachio stuck

Beignetsvia New Orleans
Cassata from the boot

Bavarian cream
through space and time from the seventeenth century hoot

riz au lait
cardamom lain

Pastel de nata
custard tart

Schwarzwälder Kirschtorte
sugar steps in black forests

Apfelstrudel waltzed
from Vienna

Sfogliatella
colored cliff hanging Amalfi sweet croissants

Madeleine
can cans

Babka
sugar bump fertility bunts

Medovik
from behind a lost iron curtain

Sernik twaróg
eaten after Turk ramshacks

Knedlíky Czech yeast
dumpling cheeks

Krapfen
the dough nut heir

Lebkuchen
bathed in honey ginger

Profiterole
poofter sandwich

Cremeschnitte
this life slice

holy cannoli
meringue towers in a crunch

Gaufre maple
smothered in Nutella

Crumble
dowsed in butter

we are the unexpected
QUEEN OF TARTS

in inns in the Czech Republic new parents may dine and sip wine
in heated taverns taking sabbatical

while leaving their newborns in their leaden strollers
blanket'd bundled

swathed mirthful
outside in the crisp December heathered snow

Vienna

Austria

Vienna is Hitler decadence

or is it Klimt's

chants and drums
in my injuries

Na-Mu-Myo-Ho-Ren-Ge-Kyo
Na-Mu-Myo-Ho-Ren-Ge-Kyo

a simple meal ginger soy garlic rice
amongst Christ's birth celebrations and Sylvester bringing in 1995

Hundertwasser is King in Vienna
molding his colorful creations into architecture

Robert Mapplethorpe's ghost was exhibiting
at the Kunst Haus Hundertwasser

where the floors wabble with the earth
uncut black cocks in power suits with naked Patti Smith Redondo Beaches

because the night and flexing Schwarzenegger
with leather black shine'd whips plugged into every orifice

remembering Vienna waltzes
of Hundertwasser's adorned Cypress homes

needles and jackoffs
near the drag addled subway toilets

huge sausages
that waltzed me all night

Budapest

Hungary

as we locked tongues

he took off my socks while he sat on the floor

rubbed my swollen feet

a gesture implanted in my love chemicals

the plasma in which the cities pass there was no door
just blood roads'pass

Gaza

we could reach orgasm as the toilets flood

I want to write *oh David my love*
but poetics refused me

hookah smell and the erect noble him
making love in PLO headquarters

we walked so no one would scream
we walked where refugees now flee

439

Gaza dust testosterone'd avenues abstracted feminine
in Israeli leer dissembler charlatans castration exeter

once I walked with Hamas

accidentally in their human forms

refugees in Jericho camp sand trapped between histories
Bedouin in our narratives

bankrupt occupied West Bank chain'd wall'd
between united nations and hypocrisy

Palestine Canaan ash Sham Levent
asleep on the world's faculties

in Amman Eduardo the Costa Rican priest needed papers for India
stayed with me in my room

he's Che bearded with revolution in his healing
he was trained in the spiritual arts of human to human epiphanies

our priest Eduardo the go to guy for Spanish prayers
and all forms of shin splint relief massages

one evening after listening to a Iraqi refugee
stuck between heartlands and heart lines having left his family back in Bush #1's Iraq

Eduardo featured himself at the door for needed intimacy between our pain painted bodies
massaging my inner thighs to release

aimlessly I traveled back 2000 years
to executions in the Roman Amphitheater of Central Amman

meandered into the Umayyad Byzantine Citadel
by mostly swollen foot from the death camps and body melting ovens of Oswiecim

India a future vagary with the somnambulistic guttural chants
of the exiled Rinpoche Monks from Tibet that live in McLeod Ganj Dharmashala

the landless
yet full and empty 14th Dalai Lama

and Gandhian rural khadi wheel spinners that worked for self reliance
against the colonial British textile makers were waiting for me

for us wandering
not in a dream

I see two melted faced women beggars
their words not words but excruciating wasteland moans

echoing out of their gaped holes
once mouths

as I would saunter by them on the way to get affordable cooked lentils
hummus and pita

their narrative skin
chemical fired

maroon blackened stretched
graphed and melted left for cremation

yet ghost kept alive long enough to send a message to any passerby
with no way to question desert sand in the streets of Amman

for *I am only going over Jordon*
I am a poor wayfaring stranger

raveling
through a world of woe

from below Gwalior India
where the antelopes leap

frantically the vultures shit giant hail sized excrement
after eating the Jain's bodies on the plateau left for sky burial

the petrified bulls
charge us

as our eyes met Delhi
with a purified smile

next to the holy cremation Ghat
where dear Gandhi had left us

Hey Ram
Rhesus Macaque monkeys abound

through the Old Delhi Gate
past the Red Fort and the Jama Masjid

the Indian railway into the Old Delhi bizarre of chai wallies and Bollywood billboards
banyan trees enmeshed with electrical and telephone wires

buying Holi colored spices and greens
exhausted smitten and kingly treated

I could not keep him from entering me repeatedly all night without protection
while *traveling a world of woe*

I wash in India buckets
dawning eyes

me exotic in rubber pale flesh
on the road side as I pilgrim

I begin to understand
I do not need much

just a bucket
a clean water pump from Earth's echoes to come clean

rows of spinners
untouchable children at the dust of Ghandi Raj Ghat Delhi

spinning khadi against empire
singing prayer *liberationally*

the dead donkey squeal of near death
twitching in the street

sleeping in cow piss in a barn
monks massaging each other

Indian trains
go missing

Indian flower'd garlands lotus jasmine *Ragamala*
orange heavily about my welcomed neck

is this my funeral
sewn in scented mala

pollinated bead mantras
un god'd in which I gallow

hosted in Raj Ghat by the 14th Dalai Lama
where Gandhi ash heap lay surrounded by machine guns and guttural sutras

I held a knife
as my palms balanced in his third eye reflected on China's plateau of self immolation

while sanctifying
me

He Rama
O'God

Gandhi ji
truth non violence

service and self reliance
smriti

we chant and drum
Namu-Myo-Ho-Ren-Ge-Kyo

ground smashing clay masala clay cups after chai walli guttural sutras
the immovability of swarms

Gandhian Harijan spinner khadi

home spun against clothe'd colonial intention

while shitting
I held on to ox horn and squat

next to the pink pigs
in the open

Vrindavan water bison float
in Krishna chant

amongst the red spittle betel nut spittoons

we crammed two of us into one seat in the 120 degree cinema to watch *Hum Aapke Hain Koun..!*

the highest grossing Bollywood film
now alert of his love

with trains that went missing
he read my palm

my moon line is long
next to the burning ghats

bodhi tree adjacent with sounds of Hindu Jazz
funeral procession of life death cycles in the twisted streets as wide as sacred cows

with bare asses on the Ganga dunes
graduating in sandalwood amongst the hollers

hashish change money rickshaw
chanted so nothing would fall

and I hibernate me **in this burning stick**
never has nothing meant more in this immovability of the **faggot swarms**

Qutb Minar
Vishnu iron enigma

pillar'd tightlipped testament
gravitate each shoulder

pashchima namaskarasana
to hand grasp behind for eternal luck

it is Stonewall everyday
on the streets of Delhi

betel nut smiles hang on one another
men blanket men unabashed

CODA

in the syllabus of marrow
the moon toasts the lucky people

for **I am the end of biology**
antifragile

poetics guillotined
on the threshing floor citadel

this is a portrait of not us
un duel'd spread in the sunlight of other

for even my pumpkins
vine gold

Influences/References

Abdoh, Reza, director. *Bogeyman*. By Abdoh, Los Angeles Theatre Center, 30 Aug. 1991, Los Angeles. Performance.

Albera, Dionigi, and John Eade, editors. New Pathways in Pilgrimage Studies: Global Perspectives. Routledge, 2017.

Andrews, Bruce, and Charles Bernstein. *The L=A=N=G=U=A=G=E Book*. Southern Illinois University Press, 2009

Baldwin, James. *Another Country* 1962.

Deleuze, Gilles, and Félix Guattari. A Thousand Plateaus: Capitalism and Schizophrenia.

Deleuze, Gilles and Félix Guattari, *Kafka: Toward a Minor Literature*. University of Minnesota Press, 1986.

Edelman, L. (2013). *Homographesis*. Routledge.

Edelman, Lee. *No Future: Queer Theory and the Death Drive*. Duke University Press, 2004.

Erasure. "Oh l'amour." *Wonderland*, Mute Records, 1986.

Glissant, Eduard. *Poetics of Relation.* Ann Arbor Univ. Of Michigan Press, 1997.

Hejinian, Lyn. The Language of Inquiry. University of California Press, 2000.

Hejinian, Lyn. *My Life*. 2002.

Mbembe, Joseph-Achille , et al. *Necropolitics / Achille Mbembe ; Translated by Steven Corcoran.* Duke University Press, 2019.

Smith, Patricia. *Incendiary Art*. Northwestern University Press, 2017.

Smith, Patti. "Horses." *Horses*, Arista, 1975.

Stephenson, Neal. *Snow Crash: A Novel*. Bantam Books, 1992.

Whitman, Walt. *Leaves of Grass*. Penguin Classics, 2017.

Brian L. Jacobs PhD. is a poet, publisher and editor. Brian grew up in Southern California and has been teaching for thirty-five years in both K-12 and college settings. He lives in Ann Arbor, Michigan and is married to Michael (Thye Peng), a Professor at the University of Michigan. Brian was the assistant to the Poet's Allen Ginsberg and Julie Patton, during his time at Naropa University in the mid 90's. During that time he walked half way around the world while on a peace pilgrimage with Buddhist monks commemorating WWII, visiting Europe, the Middle East and India. Brian is a three time Fulbright Scholar, which has allowed him to study in Brazil, where he studied its water issues; China, where he studied its vast 10,000 year history; and Japan, spending time to participate in a case study in one of its small towns near the Japanese Alps. He had also earned a National Endowment of Humanities grant to China, studying its philosophies and histories while living in Xi'an. He subsequently participated in a grant from Fund For Teachers visiting South Africa, Eswatini and Lesotho, plus earning other various grants that have taken him to places all over in the United States. He also taught teachers at a university in Fuzhou, China, for five summers under a grant from SABEH. Subsequently he has earned an Earthwatch grant to the rainforest of Ecuador to study climate change and caterpillars and a few years later earned another Earthwatch Senior Fellow Grant teaching teachers in Acadia, Maine, studying climate change and crabs. Brian has been to over a hundred countries and has visited all 50 states and is a proud vegan. Brian's poetry has been published in several publications including, *Willaim and Mary Review, Shiela-Na-Gig, Unbound Anthology, the Crank, Wet Grain, Tofu Ink Arts Press, The South Florida Poetry Journal, Progenitor Art and Literary Journal, GRIFFEL, University of Maine: Foxtail, Rip Rap, The Bangalore Review, Sunspot Lit, Anthropod, Pa'Lante, Dark Moon Lilith Press, Black Tape Press, Genre, Inky Blue/Celery, Red Dancefloor Press, Entelechy, 1844 Pine Street, Pasta Poetics, Trouble, In Parenthesis, Landlocked and Praxis.*